# The 20 British Prime Ministers of the 20th century

# Macmillan

FRANCIS BECKETT

HAUS PUBLISHING • LONDON

First published in Great Britain in 2006 by
Haus Publishing Limited
26 Cadogan Court
Draycott Avenue
London SW3 3BX

**www.hauspublishing.co.uk**



A CIP catalogue record for this book is available from the British Library

ISBN 1-904950-66-3

Designed by BrillDesign
Typeset in Garamond 3 by MacGuru Ltd
info@macguru.org.uk

Printed and bound by Graphicom, Vicenza

Front cover: John Holder

# Contents

# Part One

## THE LIFE

# Chapter 1: The House of Macmillan (1894–1914)

The Victorian Macmillans were an upwardly-mobile family. It took three generations to rise from grinding poverty to considerable wealth. Daniel Macmillan, the future Prime Minister's grandfather, was the tenth of the 12 children born to a very poor Scottish crofter who was sure that learning was the route out of poverty, and spent every penny he could scrape together on his children's education. It worked. After much struggle and hardship, in 1843 Daniel and his brother Alexander established the publishing house of Macmillan and Co, which expanded and prospered, and was to be the secure and ample financial foundation for the political career of his grandson. Daniel died in 1857, aged only 44. Alexander brought up Daniel's four children, including Harold's father Maurice Macmillan, in solid middle-class comfort in London, and he expanded the business so that by the time Maurice entered it, the Macmillans were a very wealthy family.

Maurice seems to have been a thoroughly kind and decent man, but without the drive and individualism of either his father or his son. However, his wife had both. Like Winston Churchill's father Randolph, he married a forceful American woman who, in the days when women were not supposed to have careers of her own, channelled her abilities into nurturing those of her sons. Nellie Belles, three years younger than Maurice, was born in Spencer, Indiana, in 1856, and the couple met in Paris, where she was studying music and sculpture. As befitted a wealthy family, they set up house in Cadogan Place, and had three sons, of whom Harold, born on 10 February 1894, was the youngest.

Wealthy parents in the dying days of Queen Victoria's long reign were rather distant figures who handed the day-to-day management of their children over to paid help. It was quite common for children to focus their need for love and security on their nannies, as Harold Macmillan did: the centre of his life was the fiercely patriotic Nanny Last. His father was a rather distant figure, only surfacing to agree with whatever domestic decision his wife had made. His mother's love for her children showed itself in her fierce ambition for them, which was what ensured that Harold went to Eton and Balliol College Oxford, and that when the war came, he should go into the most splendid regiment, the Grenadier Guards; and which also played a part in his marriage to the daughter of a duke.

We are all, in some ways, prisoners of our childhood, whether we cling to it or try to rebel against it, and that made Harold Macmillan a mass of contradictions. A man who craved affection, he always found it hard either to give or to ask for it, and years later, when he had children of his own, he was unable to give them the comradeship and understanding they needed. A deeply emotional man, prone to bouts of terrible depression, he dreaded shows of emotion, and the conflict brought about what seems to have been a complete nervous breakdown at the start of the 1930s. A shy man, he never got over his dread of public speaking, however much of it he did. A natural egalitarian, proud of the humble origins of his family and often in his early days dismissed as a parvenu, a *nouveau riche*, he was delighted to secure the hand in marriage of a duke's daughter and always found it hard to mix with people who were of his grandfather's class rather than his own. As Prime Minister his image of unflappability was laughably distant from the real man, and he eventually became a caricature of the Edwardian gentleman his father had been, a gift to the satirists of the 1960s. A man with the sort of instinctive loathing of poverty which often makes socialists, he was a Conservative politician all his life because, as he once put it, *I have to remember that I am a wealthy man.*

At the age of nine he was bundled off to a stern boarding prep school near Oxford called Summerfields which specialised in preparing boys for Eton. Its attraction was that it averaged five Eton scholarships a year. The method of his parting from his parents seems to us almost barbaric, but was quite standard in the upper classes in 1903. Since what he calls in his memoirs *lachrymose farewells* were considered bad form, *one of my father's clerks took me to Paddington in a four-wheeler with my trunk and my play-box, bought me a ticket and handed me over to a junior master who was conducting a number of boys to the same destination.* He wept that night, and in his three years at Summerfields he made just one friend, a boy called Gwynn. *I do not recall his Christian name. We stuck to surnames in those days.*[1]

Nor was he any happier at Eton, to which he won a scholarship. He made a few friends, one of whom accompanied him there from Summerfields and was to provide one of the great enduring friendships of his life. This was Harry Crookshank, who had spent his early childhood in Cairo as the son of a distinguished imperial administrator from an old Ulster family and his wealthy American wife. When Crookshank died, Macmillan was Prime Minister, but that did not stop him from spending hours at his friend's deathbed.

Macmillan and Crookshank were 'collegers' or 'tugs' – that

is to say, they had scholarships, which tended to give the game away: 'Tugs' were generally *nouveaux riches*, and their parents paid lower fees (though Maurice Macmillan could easily have afforded the full fees). The boys without scholarships, who were called Oppidans, generally came from old-established families, and masters tended to favour them, according to an Oppidan, Oliver Lyttelton, who became one of Macmillan's friends, because the masters were snobs: 'They conceived their role in the state to be that of training and teaching those who were likely to shape its future' so they 'wanted to have pupils from the great families'.[2]

They were both bad at games – Crookshank even worse than Macmillan. But Crookshank lasted the course at Eton. Macmillan did not. After three years, in 1909, Nellie Macmillan took her demonstrably miserable son away from the school. The reason given was ill health, and he was certainly ill several times at Eton, but years later, J B S Haldane, the distinguished Marxist biologist and geneticist, who was in the year above him at Eton, spread a rumour that Macmillan had been expelled for homosexuality. There is no other evidence for this, and the two men strongly disliked each other. Homo-

**Harry Crookshank** (1893–1961). Following military service in the First World War, Crookshank entered the diplomatic service, but soon determined on a political career instead. Elected to the Commons in 1924 as a Conservative, he held a range of junior ministerial positions under the National Government and the wartime coalition. On the formation of the Conservative administration of 1951 he was brought into the Cabinet as Minister of Health. He acted also as deputy Leader of the Commons, and moved to be Leader in 1952 until he was removed by Eden in favour of R A Butler in 1955, going to the Lords as Viscount Crookshank.

sexuality has always been the dreaded nameless vice in upper class boarding schools, and the headmaster of the time was making great efforts to root it out.

So at the age of 15, a series of private tutors was engaged to complete his education and see him safely into Balliol, and one of these was to have an enduring influence on his thinking and to become a lifelong friend. This was the famous Ronald Knox (1888–1957), part of that group of writers and thinkers who enlivened the Catholic world in the first half of the 20th century, a group which included Hilaire Belloc and G K Chesterton. Knox was then a high Anglican but was soon to convert to Roman Catholicism. Then only in his early 20s, he and Macmillan became close friends, and remained so even after Macmillan's mother ordered Knox to leave the house and never come back. The reason was Knox's growing Catholicism, which the American Methodist Nellie Macmillan could not stomach. She demanded, and did not get, an assurance that Knox would never discuss religion with her son. Unlike Knox and Chesterton, Macmillan never quite 'poped' – converted from high Anglicanism to Roman Catholicism – but there was something of the 'Chesterbelloc' about him all his life, in the languid epigrams, the love of churches filled with bells and smells, the quixotic combination of Edwardian Englishness and a concern for the underdog.

Knox – then a very young man, only five years older than his 17-year-old pupil – took to Macmillan, and was heartbroken to lose him as a pupil. 'I needn't – perhaps I can't – explain to you how much pleasure it gives me being with Harold,' he wrote to Nellie Macmillan, 'but if I bought that pleasure at the price of my own freedom of speech, I should consider it a Judas bargain.' He became Anglican chaplain at Trinity College, Oxford, where he was soon to meet his young protégé again. Macmillan himself was no less distressed, but far less inclined to allow his distress any written expression. As befits one of the great political operators of the century, he already knew instinctively that words were hostages.

In autumn 1911 Macmillan sat for a scholarship to Balliol College, Oxford, and won, not the top classical scholarship which his brother Dan had won, but a respectable minor one nonetheless. At Oxford, probably for the first time, he was happy. Many young men of his class and generation experienced their first real happiness at Oxford. A stultifying and violent public school, a severe home and a smothering mother – and then, the glorious freedom of university, where for the first time he made a host of lifelong friends, and there was no Nellie Macmillan to rein in his burgeoning friendship with Ronnie Knox. He even tried hard to conquer his shyness, and joined everything he could find to join – he seems, at one and the same time, to have been a member of a Tory club, the Canning; a Liberal club, the Russell; and the Fabian Society, the route into socialism for several upper-class young men, including the future Labour Prime Minister Clement Attlee.

The last half of 1913 and the first of 1914, before the Great War covered everything with its monstrous shadow, were perhaps the happiest few months of Harold Macmillan's life. He became secretary of the Oxford Union (and would have gone on to be president had it not been for the war) where his speeches seemed to be those of a young man moving rapidly leftwards: he spoke against public schools and in favour of 'the main principles of socialism'. He covered his shyness with a fashionably languid façade, and was suspected of modelling himself on the famously languid Conservative leader and former Prime Minister Arthur Balfour. His speeches, as reported in the Oxford undergraduate magazine

*Isis*, were elegant, learned and funny: 'Mr. M.H. Macmillan in a brilliant maiden speech ...' 'Mr Macmillan was decidedly amusing. He concluded inter alia with quotations from F.E. Smith, John Bright, G.O.M. and Macaulay ...' 'Mr M.H. Macmillan was quite brilliant in his way. His phraseology was wonderful ...'[3] He met and heard the Liberal Chancellor of the Exchequer David Lloyd George at the Union that year, and was lost in admiration for the man's oratory.

And it was that same golden year that he went to France, his first trip abroad except for a Greek cruise when he was at Eton. One of his tutors invited him to join a reading party in France: two days in Paris, then a wonderful summer in the Alps. He talked religion endlessly with Ronnie Knox, he punted and bathed and dined and talked, and passed his 'Mods' with a first. He prepared for another glorious summer in the French Alps, packing his books and going to a grand ball in London, emerging at dawn to hear a paper boy shouting 'Murder of Archduke'. But what did that have to do with the golden young man from the golden age of Edwardian England as he walked languidly through the West End in last night's dinner jacket?

It had everything to do with him. Harold Macmillan, like hundreds of other young men, rushed to enlist when they heard there was a war on. They were fearful of missing the fun, for they knew it would be all over by Christmas. He was quickly commissioned, though he had no military training at all, as befitted a wealthy young man from Eton and Oxford. But the King's Royal Rifle Corps, in which he first enlisted, was not the sort of fashionable regiment which Nellie Macmillan considered suitable for her son. Old Etonians joined the Grenadier Guards, and it was to this chic and splendid regiment that she arranged for her son to be transferred.

Life was still, he wrote afterwards, *like a perpetual garden party. Glorious weather; lots of friends from London; plenty of visits to London.* He grew the moustache which was to prove such a magnet for cartoonists 40 years later, but which, in those days, was considered to give a man's face a military aspect – so much so that Osbert Sitwell, one of Macmillan's brother officers in the Grenadiers, was instructed by his Colonel to grow one. Sitwell apparently replied: 'What colour, sir?'[4]

And there was still time for theology. Knox was soon to be received into the Catholic Church. He was sure Macmillan would come too, as his protégé had promised. But he misjudged his man. Partly, Macmillan did not want to upset his mother. Partly, perhaps, the calculating career politician was already at work: Catholics did not reach the top in British politics in those days. Whatever the reason, to Knox's bitter disappointment, Macmillan hesitated at the brink, and did not jump. He would be a High Anglican all his life.[5]

They went to war with glowing hearts – especially the Grenadiers, conscious of being an elite. It was the start of the great game of life, and like Nellie Macmillan, their first concern was that their army status should reflect their standing in society. But Macmillan, despite his family wealth, was not quite out of the top drawer. The man who, 40 years later, came almost to embody the old aristocracy, was in 1914 open to the deadly sneer of being *nouveau riche.* It was Eton's Oppidans, not its Collegers, who were going to get commissions first.

One of these, who had been friendly with Macmillan at Eton, was Robert 'Bobbety' Cranborne (1893–1972), son of Lord Salisbury and scion of the Cecils – who was to rise with Macmillan and in the end fall out bitterly with him. The Cecils were one of the most magnificent families in the land. They served the Tudor kings, after an ancestor fought alongside Henry VII at the Battle of Bosworth in 1485.

William Cecil, later Lord Burghley, and then his son, Robert Cecil, were the men on whom Elizabeth I depended above all others. Robert Cecil was created Earl of Salisbury.

The family was active and prominent in Georgian and Victorian politics, when they upheld the interests of the land-owning class and opposed parliamentary reform. Bobbety Cranborne's grandfather, Robert Gascoyne-Cecil, Lord Salisbury, was the most distinguished Cecil since Stuart times, being Prime Minister three times, his last term ending only in 1902, when, in true lordly manner, he handed the job on to his nephew, A J Balfour. It's easy to become Prime Minister, said wags, if Bob's your uncle, and the phrase entered the language.

So Lord Salisbury's son had little difficulty in securing a commission in the Grenadiers for his own son Bobbety, and for his son's friends, like another Eton Oppidan and friend and contemporary of Macmillan's, Oliver Lyttelton. It took further months of furious networking by Nellie Macmillan to achieve the same for young Harold. But she did it.

# Chapter 2: The War that Changed Everything (1915–19)

The First World War shaped a generation of politicians: the men who came to govern the country 20 or so years later. Not one of them, of any political party, could ever escape the dark shroud they lived under between 1914 and 1918; not one could forget the friends they lost, the things they saw, the physical wounds they carried, even for an instant of their lives; there was not one of them whose judgements were not permanently changed – in some cases warped – by the earthquake we know as the First World War, but which their generation called simply The Great War. It was at the root of everything that generation of men ever did or thought.

Some of them had opposed the war and been abused and assaulted by other men, and handed white feathers by women. Others – Macmillan, Clement Attlee, Hugh Dalton – fought in that most terrible of wars, and what they saw in the trenches would haunt them all their lives. The scars were not just emotional: many of them, including Macmillan, carried and felt the physical scars all their lives. They lost most of their friends, and never quite got over the sense of guilt that they had survived. It was also a great levelling experience. Lord Salisbury's grandeur, and Nellie Macmillan's wealth and networking skill, might be enough to secure commissions for their sons, but it could not protect them against the horrors of the Western Front, which they shared with the poorest of the soldiers.

In fact, the speed with which Bobbety Cranborne and Oliver Lyttelton obtained commissions put them in danger some months before Macmillan and his friend and fellow Eton Colleger Harry Crookshank joined them on the Western Front in July 1915. Second Lieutenant Macmillan realised very quickly how much better off he had been in Oxford, and tried to surround himself with books even in the trenches. *The more I live in these warlike surroundings*, he wrote to his mother, *the more thankful I am for all the traditions of the classic culture*. He saw himself as a scholar turned soldier, a race apart from the career soldiers who would have been in the army even had there been no war. As befitted a wealthy Grenadier officer, he ate and drank well in those early months of the war and was put to work to censor the men's letters home – his first introduction, and an unexpectedly moving one, to working-class culture, as he wrote to his mother: *They have big hearts, these soldiers, and it is a very pathetic task to have to read all their letters home ... There comes occasionally a grim sentence or two, which reveals in a flash a sordid family drama. 'Mother, are you going ever to write to me. I have written ten times and had no answer. Are you on the drink again, that Uncle George write me the children are in a shocking state?'*[1]

*The more I live in these warlike surroundings, the more thankful I am for all the traditions of the classic culture.*

MACMILLAN

On 27 September 1915 he was wounded for the first time. The Battle of Loos was one of those messy, incompetently led displays, in which 60,000 men were lost, for an advance of about a mile of ground gained. Macmillan's unit, under the leadership of one Captain Jummie Morrison, found itself isolated far too close to the German lines, and had to try to escape by crawling away. But, wrote Macmillan in his memoirs, *since Jummie could not crawl (he was proud and corpulent), I did not see that I could very well do so either. I therefore walked about, trying to look as self-possessed as possible, under a heavy fire.* He was shot in the head and the right hand. The bullet to his head merely concussed him, but the wound in the hand was serious, and troubled him all his life, resulting in later life in spidery handwriting and a limp handshake. But he was lucky. More than 300 Grenadiers had been killed, and the bullet to the head should have carried Macmillan off with them. He had also shown himself to be a brave officer who could keep cool under fire.

He was evacuated to hospital in Rouen, and thence for a time allocated ceremonial guard duty in London. But Easter 1916 found him in charge of a platoon near Ypres, in an exposed trench and cut off from other British forces, frightened but, in the manner of many front-line soldiers at that time, utterly, naively convinced of the moral value of the war. *I never see a man killed but think of him as a martyr*, he wrote to his mother, and he resisted her attempts to find him a safer billet away from the front line with *the much abused staff.*[2] In Ypres he was joined by his old friend Harry Crookshank.

**The 1st Regiment of Foot Guards** was founded by Charles II while in exile in the Netherlands in the 1650s. As the senior Foot Guards regiment, it served in virtually every campaign of the 18th and 19th centuries, winning the title Grenadier Guards for its defeat of the final attack by Napoleon's Imperial Guard at Waterloo in 1815. During the First World War, the regiment, which gained a fourth battalion, fought in almost all the major battles on the Western Front. Battle honours for the Marne, the Aisne, Ypres, Loos, the Somme, Cambrai, Arras, Hazebrouck and the Hindenburg Line are inscribed on the Colours of the Regiment.

The two young men found themselves in some of the worst trenches, mostly water-filled shell holes – a place the Prime Minister's son Raymond Asquith, soon to be killed, described as 'the most accursed, unholy and abominable place I have ever seen, the ugliest, filthiest, most fetid and most desolate – craters swimming in blood, dirt, rotting and swelling bodies and rats like shadows … limbs … resting in hedges' with 'the supernaturally shocking scent of death and corruption'.[3] There Macmillan was wounded in the face, but declined the chance to leave the battalion.

Ypres was a sideshow. The big push was to be on the Somme, to which Captains Macmillan and Crookshank were sent. At first it seemed a blessed relief. The trenches were comparatively habitable, and the scenery attractive. They amused themselves with each other's company as best they could, tormented by the deaths of Oxford friends. Yet Macmillan seems to have been sure he would not be killed. Soldiers, he said years later, had *a curious feeling* about it. He recalled a young officer friend who, just before going over the top, *came along and cried a little – we were only boys and he behaved very bravely – and he knew he'd be killed, and he was*.[4]

Great waves of soldiers were being flung at the German lines and slaughtered. In one advance, Macmillan was wounded for the third time, this time very seriously, in the knee and left buttock. He rolled into a shell hole and dosed himself with morphine. Meanwhile Harry Crookshank saw a shell burst a few yards in front of him and he, too, rolled into a shell hole and dosed himself with morphine. He saw a stream of blood but did not yet know that he had been castrated.

Crookshank was stretchered out after an hour, but Macmillan had to crawl until he was rescued and had no medical attention for hours. Crookshank now knew he would never father children, and he wore a surgical truss for the rest of his life. Macmillan barely survived. The wound became infected, the bullet remained lodged in his body, and his right arm and left leg never worked properly again, giving him his distinctive shuffling gait, a gift to the satirists of the 1960s. He might well have died had not Nellie Macmillan taken matters in hand, removing him from the army hospital in London to a private hospital where she could supervise his treatment. It was the end of his war. When the armistice came, he was still in hospital.

Both young men were forced back into the bosoms of their respective enveloping families. Crookshank never left his. Always a fussy man who expected things just so, his dreadful wounds left him emotionally humiliated and dejected, and he lived with his family all his life. Macmillan's growing Oxford-induced independence was lost: he became again shy, emotionally dependent on his mother, and immersed in his books. He read widely and taught himself Italian.

Like many men who had fought in the war, he found himself uncomfortable with men of his generation who had not fought. Partly it was the lack of a experience so fundamental that you could never quite relate to people who had not shared it. Partly it was the instinctive contempt for the 'gentlemen of England now abed' who 'will hold their manhoods cheap while any speak, That fought with us upon St Crispin's Day' – some of them quoted the *Henry V* speech to show what they thought of the 'conshies'. Old soldiers were bound together by what they had suffered and the friends they had lost. Even Ronnie Knox was never quite the friend, confidante and comrade he had once been.

He was sure he could not regain the happiness he had known at Oxford. That wonderful world had died for him along with all the fine things there were about being alive, young and rich in 1914. *I did not go back to Oxford after the war*, he wrote years later. *It was not just that I was still a cripple. There were plenty of cripples. But I could not face it. To me it was a city of ghosts. Of our eight scholars and exhibitioners who came up in 1912, Humphrey Sumner and I alone were alive.*[5]

It was a common feeling among the men who had fought the war. Another Old Etonian who was to become a major political figure, and Chancellor of the Exchequer in 1945, was Hugh Dalton, one of whose closest friends had been the poet Rupert Brooke. Dalton wrote in his autobiography more than three decades later: 'People have sometimes asked, since then, why I had so few men friends of my own age. The answer is the war. Before that I was very rich in friendships.'[6] Macmillan was typical of the generation in the feeling of guilt that he lived, a feeling, as he once wrote, *of an obligation to make some decent use of the life that had been spared to us*. Every man who fought on the Western Front came back fundamentally changed, fundamentally different from the generation above them which had precipitated the war but had not fought it, and from men of their own generation who had, for whatever reason, not fought. Macmillan did not make up the lost emotional ground for another 20 years, and no one who met him in the 1920s imagined for a moment that they were in the presence of a future Prime Minister – let alone one of the most successful showmen ever to have occupied 10 Downing Street.

> *To me it* [Oxford] *was a city of ghosts. Of our eight scholars and exhibitioners who came up in 1912, Humphrey Sumner and I alone were alive.*
>
> MACMILLAN

Outside the cocoon of Macmillan's private hospital and his mother's home, the world was in turmoil. Britain seemed nearer to armed revolution than at any time in its history, especially after Lloyd George's Conservative-dominated government went to the country on a patriotic ticket in a 'khaki' election, and its victory ended any thought of fundamental political change.

Macmillan, insulated by wealth from the hardships of the lives of the men he had once led, and insulated by frailty from the rough-and-tumble of political life in London, did not see that men as dreadfully wounded as he was were begging in the streets. But he did know the working man, in a way that the rich before 1914 never knew them, for he had led them, shared their dugouts and their hardships, and censored their letters home, and that knowledge was to affect his attitudes throughout his life. He was, without yet knowing it, full of political ideas which would have horrified his father, and which greatly complicated his career for the next 20 years.

But in 1919, politics did not seem like a suitable vocation for the shy, bookish young man who hobbled around London's West End, talking quietly to such old friends as were still alive – a charmless man, said people who knew him at that time, though the description seems extraordinary to those who only know the old charmer who became Prime Minister nearly 40 years later.

Old friends seemed to adjust faster to the new world – though in the long term, we can now see that they adjusted less thoroughly. Oliver Lyttelton went into the city and soon started making serious money. Bobbety Cranborne and Harry Crookshank joined the large flock of old Etonians in the diplomatic service – Crookshank by passing the examinations, and Cranborne, though he failed them, by using his family connections. Cranborne's route was the better one – he went to Paris, as an aide to his uncle Lord Robert Cecil, and worked on the drafting of the Treaty of Versailles.

What was Macmillan to do? There was of course always a job and a career for him in the family publishing firm. But where some men felt an urgent need to change the world, to make sure that the sacrifices of their friends were not in vain, Harold Macmillan seems to have felt an urgent need to be somewhere else, to be in a place not peopled by ghosts, and perhaps to be in a place not dominated by his mother.

Family connections obtained for him an offer to go to Bombay as ADC to the governor, but Macmillan's doctors vetoed the idea: the Indian climate, they said, was quite unsuitable for a man with still-suppurating wounds. But Nellie Macmillan got him another offer, to go to Canada as ADC to the Duke of Devonshire, Governor-General of Canada, through the Duke's wife, whom Nellie had met on the charity circle. He reached Ottawa in March 1919.

# Chapter 3: Years of Hope and Despair (1919–29)

In 1919 the Canadian Governor-General was a powerful figure, in many respects more important than the elected Canadian Prime Minister. Victor, ninth Duke of Devonshire, had been an important political figure in Britain, serving in government under Balfour until 1905, then again under Asquith after 1915. He had a walrus moustache, a lugubrious air, and a lively interest in politics, and was pleased to have in Captain Macmillan an intelligent, literate, politically minded young ADC who was happy to sit with him into the small hours exchanging political gossip and ideas.

The two got on – rather better, in fact, than Macmillan got on with the younger members of the Duke's entourage, who found him rather shy and serious-minded. Nonetheless, he enjoyed himself pretty well there, partly because, for the first and only time in his life, he fell in love, as Nellie Macmillan probably hoped he would do, with the Duke's 19-year-old daughter.

Whether Lady Dorothy Cavendish was ever in love with Macmillan, it is hard to know for certain. She was unlike him and all his male friends – younger, much less educated and not very well read. Daughters of the aristocracy were deemed quite knowledgeable enough if they had a working knowledge of horses and knew how to hunt. She was shrewd, certainly, but knew little of life, and virtually nothing of the conditions on the Western Front which had shaped the personality of her father's cerebral and serious ADC. She wanted to get away from her mother, for Evie Devonshire was as fearsome a matriarch as Nellie Macmillan, and she must have taken a liking at least to the clever, moustachioed, mournfully good-looking young war hero, whose shuffling walk was known to be a legacy of his bravery on the field of battle.

A striking-looking woman, warm and with a sharp sense of humour, she was fun to be with, but not intellectually exacting. She was also, as Macmillan was to find out, much keener on sex than he was. But neither of them knew that then. Macmillan, like many upper-class men of his generation, had little experience of women, for none were to be found in Eton or the Grenadiers, and very few in Oxford, and he had no sisters.

Macmillan courted her assiduously, and by the end of that year, 1919, they were engaged. The day before the wedding, in April the next year, Macmillan wrote her a letter which, we may be sure, expressed exactly what he felt: *My darling, I must write the last letter which I shall write before you become my wife. But not, dearest Dorothy, the last love letter you will get from me. For Dorothy, I shall always be your lover ... Your devoted Harold.*[1]

Their glittering society wedding in London brought Macmillan's Canadian stay to an end after just ten months, and he became one of three junior partners in the family firm alongside his older brother Dan. His first child, Maurice, was born in 1921, and the second, Catherine, four years later. Dorothy loved children, but Harold never overcame his reserve with them (or with most other people), and was always, as his own father had been, a rather distant figure. While her husband was in London working, Dorothy saw more of both her mother and her mother-in-law that she probably wanted to see. Nellie Macmillan often persuaded her to take the children to the Macmillan country house, Birch Grove, and Evie Devonshire whisked them to the vast Devonshire family estate, Chatsworth, in Derbyshire. Perhaps the freedom from her mother which she hoped for from marriage was starting to turn sour; perhaps she thought Macmillan ought to make a greater effort to be with her – he cheerfully admitted to getting away from Chatsworth as fast as he could. However it happened, these years probably created the atmosphere in which their marital problems of the 1930s developed.

For his part, perhaps the snobbery of the Devonshires alienated him more than he ever admitted. To them, Macmillan would always be a social inferior, for he was in trade, and not interested in horses. They laughed at the smart, unsuitable clothes he wore on the grouse moor. They preferred the son-in-law from another great family, Macmillan's Eton contemporary, Bobbety Cranborne. Macmillan never complained; but his son once said Chatsworth must have been 'absolute hell' for him.

At the office, the three senior partners in the firm, including Macmillan's father Maurice, were the generation above Harold and Dan. The firm was well-established, if a little stuffy. Macmillan found it perfectly agreeable, doing useful work to rationalise the printing side and taking over the handling of some of the company's big-name authors, including Thomas Hardy, Rudyard Kipling, W B Yeats and Sean O'Casey. He was personally closest to O'Casey, despite the writer's professed atheism and Marxism: in his memoirs he pronounced O'Casey and Ronnie Knox to be *saintly*. He brought the firm new authors who added to its prestige and profitability, like the historian Lewis Namier (whom Macmillan had known at Oxford). For his brother Dan, Macmillans was to be a lifetime career, as it had been for their father. But after a year or so, Harold Macmillan was already thinking seriously about a political career.

Partly this was because his mentor and father-in-law, the Duke of Devonshire, was back in the Cabinet as Colonial Secretary. He had been brought back when the Conservatives finally pulled out of Lloyd George's wartime coalition government, and Andrew Bonar Law formed a Conservative government containing no less than seven peers in a Cabinet of 16, including Bobbety Cranborne's father, Lord Salisbury. Devonshire's biggest task was to deal with a problem which he and Macmillan had discussed in those long evenings in Ottawa, and which was to come back and haunt Prime Minister Macmillan: finding a new relationship with South Africa, Rhodesia and Kenya. The white settlers wanted greater independence while not conceding any power to the black majority, or to the Boers, and were quite willing to defy the mother country in order to secure it. 'Afraid we shall have a very difficult matter with Kenya. The white settlers really make everything very difficult' complained Devonshire in his diary, in words that Macmillan might have used 40 years later.[2] Devonshire horrified the Kenyan whites with a White Paper that said: 'Primarily, Kenya is an African territory ... the interests of the Africans themselves must be paramount ... His Majesty's government regard themselves as exercising a trust on behalf of the African population.'

Macmillan liked and admired the old Duke, and shared his view of the white settlers. Not so his old Etonian friend, and now brother-in-law, Bobbety Cranborne: this enlightened attitude towards native people in Africa was hardly likely to be shared by the scion of the Cecils. Their final, terminal falling-out was still 40 years in the future, but the issue was the same one they watched their father-in-law try to settle in the 1920s: the position of the white minority in African colonies. Cranborne could not know that one day he would watch Macmillan undermine white power and break up the Empire, but he harboured a dark suspicion that Macmillan had dangerously radical views.

When he decided to stand for Parliament, Macmillan almost offered himself as a Liberal candidate. The days when you started by choosing a political career, and then chose your party, were coming to an end, but, in those elevated circles, not quite ended yet. The Liberal Party would have suited Macmillan's opinions better, but he could see that it was a fading force, and in any case, his contacts – the Devonshires, the Cecils – were far more use to a Conservative politician.

Soon after becoming Prime Minister and leading his party to victory in the 1922 general election, Bonar Law was told that he was terminally ill with cancer, and resigned. The new Prime Minister, Stanley Baldwin, was convinced that he must bring in tariffs on foreign goods to protect British industry; but the 1922 election had been won on a promise of no tariffs. So Baldwin called a further general election in 1923, in which Macmillan was the Conservative candidate for Stockton, an industrial seat in the north-east and by no means safe Conservative territory. The safest seats went either to older or to more aristocratic men.

He lost, but by the very narrow margin of 73 votes. Ramsay MacDonald became Britain's first Labour Prime Minister, at the head of a minority administration which needed Liberal support to survive, and that support was withdrawn just ten months later, in October 1924, leading to the third general election in two years. This time 30-year-old Harold Macmillan won Stockton by more than 3,000 votes. He was part of a landslide victory which gave the

Conservatives 419 seats, with 151 going to Labour and just 40 to the devastated Liberals.

If Bobbety Cranborne could have seen what Stockton was doing to his fellow Etonian's political views, he would have known years earlier than he did that the man was a bounder. Most industrial north-east constituencies had Labour MPs (with whom the young Macmillan travelled on the train to London very companionably), for the north-east was suffering dreadfully from the post-war slump, with thousands of men out of work. There was no welfare state or unemployment pay to fall back on. At any given time, between a quarter and a half of Stockton's men were out of work.

It horrified their new MP. He wrote in his memoirs: *Many men, and indeed whole families, had been without work and wages for long periods … Their clothes were worn out; their furniture in disrepair; their savings gone; their homes dilapidated … I shall never forget those despairing faces … Nor can any tribute be too great to the loyal, unflinching courage of the wives and mothers, who somehow continued, often on a bare pittance, to provide for husband and children and keep a decent home in being.*[3]

*Many men, and indeed whole families, had been without work and wages for long periods … I shall never forget those despairing faces …*

MACMILLAN

The effect on Macmillan was a little like the effect on the young Clement Attlee of going to Limehouse before the war, an experience that turned Attlee from a Conservative into a socialist. Macmillan's first reaction, like Attlee's, was individual acts of kindness – organising coach trips for children, turning a derelict shipyard into a club for the unemployed. But he soon saw, as Attlee had done, that the situation demanded a radical policy to deal with unemployment and poverty. If a mixture of family connections and colonial affairs brought him into politics, it was more than anything the search for a policy to deal with poverty that kept him there.

His concern was part of the reason why he was popular in Stockton. But also he and Dorothy took a genuine, unforced interest in the people they met there, so strange to people of their class and background. Dorothy had the precious political skill (which her husband lacked) of always remembering a face and being able to put a name to it.

Another new boy in the 1924 Conservative intake was Macmillan's old friend from prep school, Eton and the Grenadiers, Harry Crookshank. Both wanted to get on; both knew the value of their connections. As Crookshank put it with satisfaction: 'I am one of the twelve Magdelen men and one of the twelve Old Grenadiers.'[4]

But in those first few months, neither quite made the most of them. Crookshank, who had come from the Foreign Office and intended to make a mark as a foreign affairs expert, found himself overshadowed by another bright young man from the Foreign Office, Duff Cooper. And Macmillan simply did not look or sound like a man destined for high office. He was a ponderous speaker and an equally ponderous dresser, wearing a shiny top hat to the House every day right up to the Second World War, long after most MPs had abandoned them. Fellow Conservative MPs, ever so genteelly, sneered, just as the Devonshires sneered when he turned up to the grouse moors overdressed. And he would insist on banging on about the unemployed. Of course, most politicians understood that, if there was a chance of holding Stockton, Macmillan must be seen to be talking about these things – but he seemed to his fellow Conservatives rather to overdo it.

The 1926 General Strike brought into sharp relief the difference between traditional Conservatism and Macmillan. To most Conservatives, the state had no business interfering with business, and strikes – especially general strikes – were the work of the devil, or (even worse) the Communists. But the Member for Stockton had only to look round his constituency to see the suffering caused by unemployment, low wages, and the cuts in wages proposed by the mineowners, which precipitated the strike. It left him with a lifelong sympathy with trade unions. This was not something he shared with many members of his party. Years later his colleague and rival R A ('Rab') Butler described 'the dual character of the Macmillan experience, namely the soft heart for and the strong determination to help the underdog, and the social habit to associate happily with the overdog'.[5]

As he started to feel that Baldwin was being captured by the traditionalists, he grew to admire the Liberal Lloyd George; and the old statesman took to the young Conservative, calling him 'a born rebel' and giving him tips on how to improve his technically competent but rather wooden parliamentary performances. Here was Lloyd George's shrewd assessment of one of Macmillan's speeches: 'You made an essay, which was a very good essay, in an economic journal. You made about 25 points, all leading on to one another. You want to make one point, if you are a back bencher; two if you are a minister ...'[6]

There were other able young Conservative MPs who felt, to a greater or lesser extent, as Macmillan felt, and they started to meet regularly, generally over lunch, and to be identified as a more-or-less cohesive group, at first often known as the 'EYM' (Eager Young Men) and then as the 'YMCA' – the Young Men's Christian Association, a name which implied, as Simon Ball puts it, that they were 'keen but priggish'. As a publisher, Macmillan was especially useful to the group: he was able to arrange for publication of a book which would be a shop window for its members: *Industry and the State*, by Macmillan himself and three others.

Baldwin appeared to encourage the YMCA, and gave the impression of being the sort of Prime Minister with whom they could do business, prepared to consider greater state interference with industry than most traditional Conservatives. It looked as though the leading YMCAers, in particular Harold Macmillan, were rising stars, so long as the Conservative Party went their progressive way. That, of course, could not be guaranteed: *Industry and the State* was heresy in traditional Conservative circles, since it advocated a state role in industry, and the *Daily Mail* denounced it as socialism in disguise.

**Stanley Baldwin** (1867–1947) first became Prime Minister in 1923 after the resignation of Bonar Law. In 1924 he led the Conservatives to election victory over Labour, in part due to publication of the forged 'Zinoviev Letter' alleging Labour links with Soviet Russia. He faced the General Strike of 1926, but lost the election of 1929. Prime Minister again in 1935, his response to the Italian and German dictators seemed to many to be weak. After the Abdication Crisis, he resigned in 1937 at the age of 70. (See *Baldwin* by Anne Perkins, in this series.)

The YMCA's first big-name patron, rather unexpectedly, was the Chancellor of the Exchequer, Winston Churchill, who made one of its members, Robert Boothby (1900–86), his parliamentary private secretary, and asked another, Macmillan, to work for him on policies which would prevent productive industry from having to pay large sums in rates, and therefore alleviate unemployment – originally an idea of Macmillan's. It was a boost for a young politician, especially when Churchill sent one of Macmillan's papers directly to the Prime Minister. But once Churchill had announced the new scheme with a fanfare in the budget, he handed over the task of implementing it to Neville Chamberlain, who felt that Churchill had poached on his territory, and was not inclined to give any sort of role to the young politician who had aided and abetted the Chancellor. And the scheme as it finally came out was not entirely to Macmillan's liking. The young progressive wanted to see the company which actually produced things given favourable treatment over what was then called the rentier – investors, financiers and the like. It didn't happen. But the link with Churchill had been made, and was never broken.

It was one of the few things Macmillan carried out of the 1925–9 Parliament with him. For 1929 proved to be the worst year of his life. First, in the general election that year he lost his seat, Stockton returning a Labour MP as the country voted Baldwin out and elected a Labour government instead. And second, he learned that he had effectively lost his wife to another of the YMCA group, Robert Boothby.

Boothby was five years younger than Macmillan and a complete contrast to him. Where Macmillan was shy, bookish and formal, Boothby was noisy, raffish and confident. Where Macmillan was studiously overdressed, Boothby was carelessly stylish. Where Macmillan hid his lugubrious countenance behind gold-rimmed glasses and a bushy moustache, Boothby had an open, handsome face and a ready smile. Where Macmillan was dull and worthy, Boothby was handsome and a bit of a bounder. Where Macmillan was emotionally repressed and only mildly interested in sex, Boothby could make Dorothy feel loved and was as highly-sexed as she was herself. And where Macmillan had been made and broken by the war, Boothby possessed the carefree attitude which you only found in the 1920s in men who were too young to have fought in the war. Perhaps Boothby was what Dorothy Cavendish had been really looking for, as she grew up in the healthy ignorance that was deemed fitting for an attractive young woman of good family. Perhaps Boothby represented an escape from Dorothy's strong-willed and constricting mother and mother-in-law. Their love ended only with Dorothy's death in 1965. For her, it was the great romantic love of her life, and Boothby was never free – his one attempt at marriage in her lifetime was a short-lived disaster – even though she decided early on that she would not risk her husband's career by a divorce. For Boothby, it became a lifelong devotion and almost an enslavement – 'She drove me, and Harold also in a different way' – and he could never be happy with another woman. Cherie Blair writes of the affair in her book about Prime Ministers' partners: 'The liaison was widely discussed within society ... but not a word got out to the wider public. Newspaper proprietor Lord Rothermere, a close friend of Boothby's, must have known but newspapers then were discreet about private affairs.'[7]

For Macmillan it was the dark cloud which overshadowed the rest of his life. On top of the sense of loss – he never ceased to love his wife – there was loneliness and humiliation. Dorothy was a good political wife, always there when required for public and constituency occasions, but her time and her emotions were spoken for elsewhere. In a way that would be impossible now, it was kept out of the papers, but known about by the whole Westminster village. Not only that: everyone knew that the fourth and last of the Macmillan children, Sarah, was in fact Boothby's daughter, though Sarah herself went through her childhood believing that she was, like her brother and two sisters, Macmillan's daughter. Many years later, when Macmillan was dead, the Irish actress Eileen O'Casey – who was married to Sean O'Casey, a Macmillan and Co author – said that she had had a brief affair with Macmillan during the early stages of the Boothby affair. If so, it was certainly brief, and she said he was not much interested in sex. She was never the love of his life, as Boothby was the love of Dorothy's life, but she remained one of Macmillan's friends. It is hard today to imagine the self-control and inner self-sufficiency that went into living the rest of Macmillan's life, but certainly, at least for the next decade, Harold Macmillan was not a happy man.

# Chapter 4: The Coming of Another War (1929–39)

Harold Macmillan entered the 1930s at a very low ebb – perhaps the lowest of his life. Just five years earlier he had entered upon a blissful marriage with a woman with whom he was deeply in love, and upon a political career for which he clearly possessed the necessary intellect, connections and personality. Now, in one dreadful year, 1929, he had lost his wife and the basis of his political career, his seat in Parliament.

As Ramsay MacDonald formed his second Labour government, still without an overall Commons majority but this time as the leader of the largest single party, Macmillan watched miserably as old friends returned to the House of Commons. The Labour MP Hugh Dalton claimed he saw Macmillan in tears after the result, and certainly he seems to have felt like a little boy excluded from a party to which all his friends have been invited, staring unseen through the windows at the junketing within. Harry Crookshank was still inside. So, now, was Bobbety Cranborne, who had stayed out of the previous Parliament in order to devote himself to building up the family fortune in the City, and now, when he was ready to enter Parliament, had been gifted with a safe seat as befitted the scion of the Cecils.

Losing his seat was bound to be a disappointment – but it should not have been as shattering as it seems to have been.

He was a rich man. That meant, not just that he would never have to worry about money, but also that he was not going to be short of a seat in future. An able young man with money for the election fund could generally get a seat. Anyway, there would always be a job for him at the family firm. He seems not to have considered this as a long-term option, though he was active in the firm during the 1930s, playing a central part, along with his mother, in its lucrative purchase of *Gone with the Wind*.

It seems likely that he made much of his unhappiness about losing his seat in order not to talk about his real heartbreak, the loss of his wife. He could see that getting his wife back was not possible – their marriage was now for show, and for political respectability – so he wisely concentrated on the possible: finding a seat. His personal unhappiness certainly made political success that much more important to him. He must get back into Parliament. And next time, he should get a safe seat. Ambitious politicians avoid getting saddled with marginals.

The Conservatives of Hitchin in Hertfordshire, which always returned a Conservative MP, approached him because the sitting member, Major Guy Kindersley, wanted to retire. But Macmillan's radicalism scuppered that. He still held strongly the belief – regarded as heresy in the Conservative Party – that unemployment was the government's affair. When Sir Oswald Mosley resigned from the Labour Cabinet because it would not implement his proposal for a major programme of public works to tackle unemployment, Macmillan wrote to *The Times* not only supporting Mosley's proposal but also criticising Baldwin's government for failing to tackle unemployment. Kindersley told Macmillan not to do it again, or he would keep the seat himself; Macmillan refused to back down, and Kindersley announced he would indeed fight the seat again.

Mosley, the man to whose defence Macmillan had sprung, sparkled brightly for a few short weeks before immolating himself in his creation, the New Party, which was soon to become the British Union of Fascists. A few Labour MPs went with him, along with one Ulster Unionist, but in the end no Conservatives, though Macmillan had briefly been part of the Mosley circle. Breaking with Mosley, Macmillan recruited Mosley's aide, Allen Young, a former Marxist, as his research assistant. A lot of Labour people by now liked Macmillan, much better than his Conservative colleagues liked him: the future Labour Prime Minister Clement Attlee described him in a private letter to his brother as 'a good chap'.[1]

Fortunately, Stockton still wanted him – the town's Labour Party had grown very fond of the Macmillans – and did not mind the stringent conditions he laid down for going back to them: he could not promise to bind himself to Stockton for more than one election, after which he might need to seek a constituency nearer London, he told them. And they need not expect to see as much of him and Lady Dorothy as before. But before he could fight an election there, the strain which this intensely self-contained and buttoned-up

**Sir Oswald Mosley** (1896–1980) first entered Parliament in 1918 as a Conservative, but then sat as an independent before joining the Labour Party in 1924. He resigned from the government in 1930 and founded the New Party, which became the British Union of Fascists (BUF) in 1932. Initially gaining support from among others the press baron Lord Rothermere, violence at a BUF rally at Olympia in 1934 fatally damaged Mosley politically. Interned during the War for his links to Italian and German fascism, he attempted to exploit racial tensions in 1950s Britain, but retired from politics in 1966. He died in Paris in 1980. (See *Life&Times: Mosley* by Nigel Jones.)

man had been suffering for two years brought on what seems to have been a nervous breakdown. It is hard to overstate how bad a state he was in. Years later an old family nanny hinted at a suicide attempt, and Lord David Cecil, Bobbety Cranborne's brother, recalled him despairingly banging his head on the wall of a railway compartment. Nellie Macmillan stepped in, sending him for several months to a sanatorium near Munich. From there he wrote to Nellie that he would make the effort to come back if there were an election, even though the doctors were not sure he could stand the strain. His letter makes it clear that he was using politics as an escape from personal troubles: *I want to get into the H of C, because I think it wd make my life much easier.*

*I want to get into the H of C, because I think it wd make my life much easier.*
MACMILLAN

So it was again as MP for Stockton that Macmillan returned to Parliament at the 1931 election. The Labour government had imploded at the impact of the financial crisis of 1931. Ramsay MacDonald believed that the only way to prevent an immediate and devastating financial collapse was to take a loan from an American bank, and fulfil the terms dictated by the bank, which included a cut in the already very low rates of unemployment benefit, at a time of sharply rising unemployment. Macdonald's Cabinet would not agree to this, but Macdonald and two of his Cabinet colleagues combined with the Conservatives to form a National Government – in effect a Conservative government. The new government called an election, asked the country for what it called a 'doctor's mandate', and swept to victory with 556 seats and a majority over all other parties of 500. The Labour Party was reduced to just 46 seats. No wonder Macmillan won Stockton back.

But it was not a happy or a successful parliament for him. Apart from being unhappy, he was politically out of tune with the Conservative benches, his patron Churchill was out of favour and out of office (and anyway so close to Dorothy's lover Robert Boothby that Macmillan could hardly see one without the other, and he had no wish to see Boothby). Political advancement seemed further away than ever. 'He is clever,' wrote fellow Conservative MP Cuthbert Headlam in his diaries, 'and takes infinite pains to make himself well-informed, but ... he bores people too quickly and has little or no sense of humour.' Invited to stay at Birch Grove for a weekend, Headlam noted: 'The gloom of H. Macmillan is something quite terrible but he is a much disappointed man ... he is not a cheering companion even for a weekend.'[2]

With a huge parliamentary majority, his colleagues were not inclined to have much patience with the sort of left-wing ideas Macmillan was increasingly drawn to. The hunger marches of the 1930s brought to London a set of people of whose privations most Conservative MPs knew nothing, and in which they never really believed. But Macmillan knew – he had seen the suffering of the unemployed in Stockton. Its shipyards were collapsing, and many of its children were suffering from malnourishment. Unemployment, it seemed to him, was the major scourge of the time, the first matter a responsible government ought to address. Few Conservative MPs agreed.

In 1932 he took Allen Young with him on a visit to the Soviet Union, and they wrote a book on their return called *Reconstruction*, widely seen as an apologia for state planning, and – in the spirit of the times – denounced by the right as communism, and by the left as fascism. Friedrich Hayek, later to be Margaret Thatcher's favourite economist, called it a blueprint for the destruction of liberty. Three years later, with 14 other Conservative MPs, Macmillan wrote *Planning for Employment*. So by 1935, when the ageing Ramsay MacDonald finally resigned as Prime Minister to be replaced by the Conservative leader Stanley Baldwin, and another general election saw the Conservatives safely returned and Macmillan back as Stockton's MP, he had become a fringe character in the Conservative Party.

Yet, though he was a parliamentary rebel, and so close to the left that it almost amounted to apostasy, socially he was a Tory through and through, emphatically a wealthy product of Eton and the Brigade of Guards. He and Bobbety Cranborne invited each other for an all-male shooting holiday every year on their respective estates, and in London his social life revolved around the clubs – the Beefsteak, which he liked best, and Pratts, the exclusive club (his Cavendish connections got him in) which women were forbidden even to telephone.

In the second half of the 1930s, as another great war slowly turned from a terrible nightmare into something like a terrible inevitability, Harold Macmillan had ceased to look like a young man with a future, and started to look like an early middle-aged man who might have had a future, once. The party's rising star, and the man to whose flag Macmillan rallied in the second half of the decade, was three years younger than him. Another old Etonian and First World War officer, Anthony Eden (1897–1977) got his first ministerial job in 1931, aged only 34, as Under-Secretary for Foreign Affairs. In December 1935 the Foreign Secretary Sir Samuel Hoare, was forced to resign, because he had entered into a secret deal with the French Prime Minister Pierre Laval which allowed Mussolini a free hand to overrun Abyssinia, and the deal became public. Eden became Foreign Secretary. He was 39. Macmillan was 42.

As soon as the Nazis came to power in Germany in 1933, Macmillan knew he was in that section of the Conservative Party that wanted to stop Hitler, not in the Chamberlain faction which wanted to appease Hitler. He understood the other view. He knew the horror of war; his wounds still troubled him. He understood that the rise of Hitler was at least partly Britain's fault, writing in 1936: *We have an uneasy conscience about Germany. We are not happy about the Treaty of Versailles … We remember what we refused to Liberal Germany and have been forced to allow to Totalitarian Germany. We remember the humiliations of* [German chancellors] *Stresemann and Bruning; and we wonder how far we have been responsible for the triumph of Hitler.*[3] He predicted war in 1940 or 1941. He was not far out.

1936, the year that the Hoare Laval Pact parachuted Anthony Eden into the Foreign Secretary's job, was the worst year Macmillan had known since he first realised he had lost his wife to Robert Boothby. First, he was shocked to the core by the pact, and despaired of government foreign policy. He resigned the whip, along with just one other MP, Vyvyan Adams, a younger and much newer member who never, before or after, held ministerial office. This was a very extreme step to take, and he must have realised that it could easily destroy any political future he might have. That year too, the Spanish Civil War broke out, another potential area of conflict between Macmillan and his leaders. And that year saw the last of the hunger marches, a reminder of how little he had achieved in economic policy, for they were held to protest against two further measures designed to lower the rates of unemployment pay yet further. And that year, his father Maurice Macmillan died, and so did his uncles George and Frederick. The generation ahead of Harold had gone, and he would have to start putting in more time in the office, though his brother Daniel took the main burden of running the firm. The next year Nellie Macmillan died – a much greater blow, especially since Macmillan's domestic circumstances had made him more dependent than ever on his loyal, iron-willed mother.

She had found his apparently wayward politics puzzling, though she always supported him. She would have been amazed had she lived another year, for in 1938 he and Allen Young wrote *The Middle Way*, advocating deficit budgeting, spending the nation's way out of recession, centralised economic planning, nationalisation of the coal mines, a programme of public works to deal with unemployment in the short term, and bringing *the economic system under conscious direction and control ... The increased production should be directed towards raising the standard of living and security of all the people.* It proposed a minimum wage – an idea whose time did not come for another six decades. It even said: *The whole trend of development is in the direction of greater integration and the supersession of unrestrained competition by methods of co-operation.* 'Mr Harold is a dangerous pink' said the loyal Macmillan nanny, and no wonder. Baldwin was not the only Conservative leader to whom the idea of getting rid of competition – the market – and replacing it with co-operation and a planned economy was the ultimate heresy.

*'Mr Harold is a dangerous pink.'*
MACMILLAN'S NANNY

These were not new ideas – the economist John Maynard Keynes was a major influence – and they reflected much of the thinking behind Franklin Roosevelt's New Deal in the USA. But coming from a Conservative MP, they were startling. He did not seek to trim them so as to avoid offending his colleagues; in fact, he rather rubbed their noses in it, telling the House of Commons: *Unemployment is not in itself a harmful thing. When it is unemployment of the upper classes it is called leisure. The real problem is that of not having enough money.*

Macmillan returned to the fold of Conservative MPs

early in 1938, just two years after resigning the whip, when Chamberlain replaced Baldwin as Prime Minister, apparently believing that Chamberlain would provide a stronger foreign policy and a more compassionate domestic policy. In February that year Eden and his under-secretary, Macmillan's friend Bobbety Cranborne, resigned. It was the culmination of a long war of attrition between Eden and Chamberlain over foreign policy. Chamberlain's fixer, a shadowy former spy called Sir Joseph Ball, secretly funded from Conservative Central Office a magazine called *Truth*, edited by such far-right figures as the Rothermere anti-Semite Collin Brooks and the neo-fascist Henry Newnham, which Ball used to leak anti-Eden stories to the rest of Fleet Street. Ball created for Chamberlain almost a shadow foreign office, with his own private channels to the Italian government, and Chamberlain used Lord Halifax as an alternative emissary to Hitler and his sister-in-law, the widow of his older half-brother Austen, as an emissary to Mussolini. When Eden and Chamberlain met Count Grandi, Mussolini's ambassador in London, Grandi noted with amusement that they acted like 'two enemies confronting each other'. In July 1937 Chamberlain had written a personal letter to

**Neville Chamberlain** (1869–1940) was Minister of Health and Chancellor of the Exchequer in the Conservative administrations of the 1920s, and returned as Chancellor in the National Government under Baldwin in 1931. He succeeded Baldwin as Prime Minister in 1937. His reputation has been damaged by his policy of appeasement of Hitler, particularly over the Munich Agreement of 1938. He declared war on Germany in 1939, but resigned after failing to secure a sufficient majority in a confidence vote in Parliament after the invasion of Norway. He died of cancer later that year. (See *Chamberlain* by Graham Macklin, in this series.)

Mussolini and noted in his diary: 'I did not show my letter to the Foreign Secretary, for I had the feeling that he would object to it.' It was not a situation between Prime Minister and Foreign Secretary which could last.

Eden and Cranborne hoped to build an alliance with the USA, which they saw as being the only chance of averting war, and the best chance of winning a war. But when the approach from President Roosevelt they had been working for finally came – a proposal for a world disarmament conference – Eden was on holiday, and Chamberlain turned it down without consulting anyone at the Foreign Office. Eden and Cranborne were furious. Eden still hoped to reach a compromise with Chamberlain, but Cranborne was determined that they both had to resign. They were hampered in their resignation speeches by not being able, for reasons of diplomatic protocol, to tell the story of the Roosevelt approach. In the debate that followed, Macmillan was one of about 20 anti-appeasement rebels. Lord Halifax moved into Eden's job, and one of the new younger men into Cranborne's: a first step on the career ladder for Rab Butler.

Macmillan had been becoming more and more a fringe figure, organising ginger groups, talking to the exile Winston Churchill, pressing on increasingly sceptical Conservative colleagues his ideas about rapid rearmament and a planned economy. But now, with Eden and Cranborne joining him in the wilderness, he was at least part of the mainstream of malcontents. Seeing Eden and Macmillan at dinner, a Tory peer who disliked them both commented: 'Macmillan MP kept pumping sedition into [Eden's] ear. This seemed to be agreeable to Eden and every now and then one could see a wicked, vindictive gleam in his eye.' But Macmillan was shocked by what Eden's resignation told him of a Prime Minister of whom he had entertained high hopes, and when he saw Churchill, he found the great exile *almost in despair over the catastrophe.*

The next month, March 1938, saw Hitler's invasion of Austria, and Czechoslovakia was next on his list. Chamberlain flew to meet Hitler three times, the last at the famous Munich conference in September 1938, with Mussolini and the French premier Daladier, after which Chamberlain proclaimed 'peace with honour'. Macmillan played a key behind-the-scenes role among the anti-appeasement Conservatives. He was not only the link between Eden's group and Churchill's group, but also the link the with the Labour opposition, working mostly through his fellow old Etonian Hugh Dalton, but this came to nothing, because in the end only Churchill and Macmillan were prepared to make common cause with the opposition against their own leader. Macmillan courted political death by supporting, at an Oxford by-election, the anti-appeasement candidate, Dr A D Lindsay, over the official Conservative, despite threats of withdrawal of the whip, an official Tory candidate to be run against him at Stockton at the next election, and ejection from the Carlton Club.

The Churchill group was far more strident than the Eden group and Macmillan was with Churchill. He wanted a government of national unity under Churchill, and was, wrote Harold Nicholson, 'enraged that Chamberlain should stay on. He thinks that all we Edenites are too soft and gentlemanlike. That we should have clamoured for Chamberlain's removal.'[4]

Yet there was a guilty part of Macmillan that still hoped to avoid war. He remembered what war had done to his own youth. Even at the time of Munich, though he rejected the humiliating terms to which Chamberlain had assented, he later recalled thinking: *My son would stay at school and go to Oxford in the autumn*. But he knew war was on its way, and he never wavered in his view that Britain ought to have fought at the time of Munich. The war came on 1 September 1939, and if the First World War had broken Harold Macmillan, the Second World War was to make him.

## Chapter 5: The Ruler of the Mediterranean (1940–5)

In 1940, Churchill and Eden returned to government, Churchill as First Lord of the Admiralty and Eden as Dominions Secretary. And 19-year-old Maurice Macmillan left Oxford and joined the army, just as his father had done in 1914. Lady Dorothy Macmillan busied herself looking after child evacuees and Czech exiles to whom the Macmillans had given over Birch Grove.

But what was Harold himself to do? *I was too old to fight*, he wrote later. *I had already tried to get back into the Reserve Battalion of my regiment, but they did not want officers of my age and physique ... I held no post, even in the lowest ranks of the administration ...* He managed to grab a small piece of the action in January 1940 when the Soviet Union invaded Finland. A committee was formed, with government support, to try to help Finland. Macmillan was invited to serve on it, and to travel to Finland, where he arrived on 12 February in a white fur hat which was to re-emerge 20 years later when he visited Russia as Prime Minister. From Finland, he deluged the Prime Minister with telegrams urging immediate aid.

Finnish resistance, outgunned and outnumbered, collapsed on 13 March. Chamberlain told the House of Commons that 'no appeal that was made to us by the Finnish government remained unanswered' but Macmillan was able to show this was untrue. *We could only send 25 howitzers out of 150 asked for; only 30 field guns out of 166 asked for, and these were despatched one month after the request*. In a performance which was far more effective than he had been in the House for some time, he attacked the government for incompetence, and he helped found a group of anti-Chamberlain Conservatives called the 'Watching Committee'.

The Watching Committee found soulmates in other parties. The Labour leader Clement Attlee disliked Chamberlain and believed he was the wrong man to fight the war. He asked pointedly how Britain could still have 900,000 unemployed after eight months of war. A leading Liberal, and future Liberal leader, Clement Davies, convened secret meetings between Labour leaders and dissident Conservatives aimed at a joint initiative to get rid of Chamberlain.

In April Germany invaded Denmark and Norway. British resistance, improvised and badly organised, collapsed quickly. Attlee knew the moment had come to pounce: 'The government are not organising the resources of this country ... To win the war we want different people at the helm from those who have led us into it.' Lloyd George, in his last big parliamentary speech, said: 'The Prime Minister should give an example of sacrifice, because there is nothing that can contribute more to victory in this war than that he should sacrifice the seals of office.' Leo Amery, one of Macmillan's Watching Committee, famously echoed Oliver Cromwell: 'You have sat here too long for any good you have been doing. Depart, I say, and let us have done with you. In the name of God, go!'

*'You have sat here too long for any good you have been doing. Depart, I say, and let us have done with you. In the name of God, go!'*

LEO AMERY (AFTER OLIVER

Thirty-three Conservatives including Macmillan voted

against the government and 60 more abstained. The government majority was cut from 200 to 81. Macmillan, who had lobbied tirelessly among Conservative MPs, sang a chorus of *Rule Britannia* with Labour MP Josh Wedgwood in the lobby. So on the day that Germany invaded Holland and Belgium, Westminster was entirely absorbed with its own affairs. Chamberlain, though he struggled against the inevitable, would have to go. Who was it to be – Churchill or the Foreign Secretary Lord Halifax? Macmillan had long ago hitched himself to the Churchill bandwagon; he and the rest of the Watching Committee saw Halifax as a part of the old regime, irrevocably compromised by appeasement. Chamberlain summoned Halifax and Churchill. Churchill wrote later: 'He told us that he was satisfied that it was beyond his power to form a National Government. The response he had received from the Labour leaders left him in no doubt of this. The question therefore was whom he should advise the King to send for after his own resignation had been accepted … As I remained silent, a very long pause ensued. It certainly seemed longer than the two minutes which one observes in the commemorations of Armistice Day. Then at length Halifax spoke. He said that he felt his position as a peer, out of the House of Commons, would make it very difficult for him to discharge the duties of Prime Minister in a war like this … He spoke for some minutes in this sense, and by the time he had finished it was clear that the duty would fall upon me – had in fact fallen upon me.'[1]

It was to be a coalition government. Swiftly Churchill and Attlee decided they were not going to waste any time bargaining over Cabinet posts. There was to be a small War Cabinet, as the Macmillan group wanted: three Conservatives, Churchill, Chamberlain and Halifax, and two Labour men, Attlee and his deputy Arthur Greenwood. Only Halifax, the

Foreign Secretary, should have a departmental responsibility, though Attlee was to be Lord Privy Seal, and Churchill took the title of Minister of Defence. Labour should have a little over a third of the posts in the government.

Eden became Secretary of State for War. Bobbety Cranborne became Paymaster General in deference to his distinguished lineage, even though his health was too poor to allow him to do much work. Macmillan lobbied despairingly for a job, getting Leo Amery and even Robert Boothby to speak to Churchill for him, and after a few days, when the Prime Minister at last got down to the junior appointments, he became parliamentary secretary to the Ministry of Supply. He was 46 and it was his first government job. For two key jobs Churchill went outside politics. The newspaper proprietor Lord Beaverbrook became Minister of Aircraft Production, and Ernest Bevin, General Secretary of the Transport and General Workers Union, became Minister of Labour and National Service.

Chamberlain's resignation later that year (he was dying of cancer) gave Churchill the chance of a reshuffle in October, bringing a government job for Macmillan's old Eton and Grenadiers contemporary Oliver Lyttelton as President of the Board of Trade. Lyttelton, like Beaverbrook and Bevin, was not a politician but a City broker. The little matter of finding him a seat in Parliament was dealt with by Bobbety Cranborne, whose cousin, the MP for Aldershot, agreed to go to the House of Lords. With Cranborne himself promoted to the Cabinet as Dominions Secretary, Harry Crookshank as Financial Secretary to the Treasury, and Macmillan clinging to the lowest rung of government, the Eton and Guards quartet seemed to be moving upwards in a steady and stately manner.

Under Churchill, the rules of the political game were

different. He had been out of office for a long time, and had grown reliant on his own entourage – people like Beaverbrook and the founder of the *Financial Times*, Brendan Bracken. He did not have to consult Conservative colleagues about appointments, and rarely did so; he needed Attlee far more, and consulted him far more. Those Tory rebels who had stuck with Churchill in the wilderness years had their reward, but a short-lived attempt by Macmillan and some other junior people in the government to influence strategy ceased abruptly when Churchill told Amery that if anyone wanted to criticise the government, they should resign.

The Chamberlainites resented Churchill bitterly; on his first day as Prime Minister, when he promised the House of Commons 'blood, sweat, toil and tears', only Macmillan and his friends from the Conservative benches joined Labour and Liberal MPs in cheering. Most Conservatives sat sullenly silent behind him for nearly two months, and some of them for much more than that. Churchill might be the man the country needed, but he was still a bounder, the man who had 'ratted' by changing party, not one but twice. Even to this day, traditional Conservative historians trace the decline of traditional conservatism, which culminated in the Macmillan premiership, to the perfidious Winston. Andrew Roberts says: 'In November 1917 Churchill watched Clemenceau from the diplomatic box in the French chamber and saw "all around him was an assembly which would have done anything to avoid having him there, but having put him there felt they must obey". The same may be said of Churchill and the Conservative Party in May 1940.'[2]

Three weeks after the formation of the new government, Britain was scooping its exhausted army from Dunkirk's beaches. A fortnight later, on 17 June 1940, the new French government of Marshal Petain asked Hitler for an armistice, and Britain faced a summer of German bombing and the near-certainty of invasion. Today people talk about 'the Dunkirk spirit' as though it was one of unalloyed heroism. But the soldiers felt let down, both by the French army and by their own leaders. They had not been trained or equipped to withstand being shelled, dive-bombed and machine-gunned by low-flying aircraft, night and day. Civilians looked sourly at the sacrifices which were to be demanded of them, and asked whether the rich would this time be making the same sacrifices. Mass Observation took the temperature of civilian morale. Its reports were full of verbatim quotes like 'It looks as though all we can do is give up. It's no use throwing away lives when there's no hope.' Hitler had swallowed Denmark, Norway, Holland, Belgium, Luxembourg and France, and Britain was next on his menu.

It fell to the Ministry of Supply to replace all the weapons which had been left behind on the beaches of Dunkirk, and to supply a hugely expanded army with those weapons in a matter of weeks. It was a huge task, and Macmillan thought his boss, Labour's Herbert Morrison, was not up to it. Morrison, Macmillan told friends, was *no good* and *the meanest man I know*. He was so physically cowardly (Morrison had been a pacifist in the First World War, and the old distrust between soldiers and 'conshies' never quite left that generation) that as soon as it was dark, he went straight to the ministry dugouts and did not emerge until morning.[3] Macmillan loathed the dugout, and throughout the Blitz he slept in his rooms in Piccadilly, joining Dorothy in Sussex for some weekends. When the Piccadilly rooms were blown up, he moved to a flat belonging to one of his authors, Hugh Walpole.

Morrison, said Macmillan, thought more about publicity than armaments. But Morrison, in his memoirs, wrote of Macmillan: 'In his loyalty to me, his advice for my advancement tended to occupy his mind to such an extent that I had to remind him that we had a war job to do and that personal careers were not important.'[4] What sort of conversations ended with each man thinking he had dragged the other away from personal concerns and back to the matter in hand? Macmillan's account was probably nearer the truth. The idea that his personal career was unimportant was not one that anyone ever associated with Morrison.

Morrison went to the Home Office five months later, and was replaced by Sir Andrew Duncan, whom Macmillan found *cautious, diligent, orderly, unimaginative, but efficient*. The rapid change of ministers made Macmillan more important than the usual parliamentary secretary, and Supply was a task to which his talents and his political thinking suited him very well, for if ever there was a task which required centralised state planning, with industry and government working hand in hand, this was it.

On 22 June 1941, Hitler invaded the Soviet Union, and Macmillan's ministry was called on to send huge quantities of arms and munitions to Britain's new ally. To meet the new challenge Churchill drafted in Lord Beaverbrook. Politicians related to Beaverbrook in two ways. Either they were fascinated by him, as Michael Foot always was, and became part of his inner circle; or they were repelled by him, as Clement Attlee was. Attlee thought Beaverbrook one of the few genuinely evil men he ever met, and when Beaverbrook died, Attlee refused to write an obituary, saying he could think of nothing good to say about him. Macmillan tended towards the Attlee camp: *He couldn't resist seducing men in the way he seduced women. And once a man was seduced by him, he was finished. I've seen one or two people ruined by it*. But he differed from Attlee in thinking Beaverbrook a great man despite it all: *He radiated strength, authority, determination and energy*. And he thought Beaverbrook was good for Churchill: *Max recharged the old boy's batteries.*[5] He established a good relationship with the press baron which paid dividends years later when Macmillan was Prime Minister.

In February 1942 Macmillan moved from Supply to be Under-Secretary at the Colonial Office. It was a modest promotion, but contemporaries were leapfrogging him. The high-flyers seemed to be men like Rab Butler, eight years younger than Macmillan and given the post of Minister of Education at the same time as Macmillan went to the Colonial Office. Macmillan's boss was his Eton friend and contemporary Bobbety Cranborne, now Lord Salisbury following his father's death. Harry Crookshank was offered, and refused, the job of Minister of Works and a key role in thinking about post-war reconstruction, along with a peerage. It seems especially to have upset Crookshank that Churchill should have offered him a peerage when Churchill knew Crookshank's terrible secret – that his testicles had been blown off in the First World War, and what use was a hereditary peerage to a man who could never father children?

Yet despite appearances, Macmillan was on the up escalator and Cranborne and Crookshank on their way down. Churchill had the two latter marked down as members of the Eden circle, for which he was coming to have something like contempt, believing that the Edenites were far too gentlemanly. He had identified Macmillan as someone with backbone, along with Macmillan's other Eton and Grenadiers contemporary, Oliver Lyttelton, whom Churchill sent to be Minister Resident in Cairo to handle all the political and diplomatic work so that the generals could get on with the fighting – a task at which he so impressed the Prime Minister that when he recalled him, it was to take over the Ministry of Munitions with a seat in the War Cabinet. There, Lyttelton started to lose his glamour.

His political inexperience started to show. A couple of gaffes – minor, but the sort that a safe pair of hands is not expected to make – took the gloss off his reputation. Macmillan, on the other hand, had been around far too long and had struggled far too hard to start making mistakes now.

The war was going badly right up to victory at El Alamein in October 1942, and two months later, on 31 December, Macmillan was sent to Algiers to be Minister Resident at Allied Force Headquarters, with Cabinet rank but not in the War Cabinet, reporting direct to the Prime Minister – Churchill's safe pair of hands in a difficult situation. He took with him his young private secretary from the Ministry of Supply, John Wyndham, who was to stay with him for many more years and become one of his closest confidantes.

The Americans did not mind Churchill having a representative there, but they thought he should simply be attached to the US commander General Dwight D Eisenhower's staff. 'What have you come for?' Eisenhower asked Macmillan coldly on his first day in Algiers in January 1943. Macmillan told Eisenhower that his mother came from Indiana, and within a few days Eisenhower had quite taken to the upper-crust English politician. Macmillan also managed to break down the suspicion of his American counterpart, Robert Murphy, and ensured that he had an office next door to Murphy's. His method of dealing with the Americans was to make them feel they were in charge: *This way you could often get them to do what you wanted, while they persuaded themselves it was really their idea*, he wrote in his memoirs.

The big political problem he had to solve was to find one French leader – and only one – under whom the French could unite and who could win over the French colonies for the Allies. The Americans loathed the prickly Free French leader General de Gaulle. President Roosevelt wanted to find another French leader to support, while de Gaulle was determined to establish himself as the sole leader of the French liberation forces, and leader of a government-in-waiting. He saw Macmillan as the mouthpiece of an Anglo-American plot against him. Macmillan was walking a political tightrope – and discovering, to his great pleasure, that it was something he had a real talent for.

Macmillan told Murphy how much de Gaulle's determination to carry on the fight had meant to Britain in her darkest hours, and he persuaded Churchill to see the French general's point of view. He told Churchill that if the Germans had successfully invaded in 1940 and Churchill had gone to America and built a government in exile, Churchill would have behaved as de Gaulle was now behaving: *We would have felt it necessary to be ultra rigorous about the rights of the British empire.* Churchill said: 'Yes, I see that.' Macmillan was de Gaulle's best ally, though de Gaulle himself did not always realise it.

**General Charles de Gaulle** (1890–1970) commanded a tank formation during the German invasion of France, and was briefly appointed War Minister before the Pétain government sought an armistice in June 1940. He established himself as the leader of the Free French in London, and was appointed President in 1945 after the liberation. Out of power until 1958, he returned as President during the Algerian crisis. He oversaw the French retreat from Empire and the break with the USA and NATO, until student unrest and the loss of a referendum lead to his resignation in 1969. (See *Life&Times: De Gaulle* by Julian Jackson.)

At the Churchill-Roosevelt summit in Casablanca with Eisenhower and Murphy, to hammer out an Allied war strategy, Macmillan's task was to get a coherent and agreed policy of dealing with the French, mediating between de Gaulle on one side and Churchill and Roosevelt on the other.

He worked hard at it, partly because he was convinced that de Gaulle was a far better leader than the only other possible candidate, General Giraud. But in order to keep de Gaulle in the game at all, he had to find a way of temporarily yoking the two together. Giraud, Macmillan wrote later, accepted every formula offered without a murmur, while de Gaulle turned them down one after the other. At last Macmillan resorted to telling the world that Churchill and Roosevelt were at Casablanca (the meeting had been kept secret until then) and arranging a photo-call at which de Gaulle and Giraud shook hands *with the best approach to a smile that they could manage*, as Macmillan wrote afterwards. Back in Algiers, Macmillan continued to guard de Gaulle's back (not an easy task, for Roosevelt had come away from Casablanca implacably opposed to the prickly general) and to try to control the General (a virtually impossible task).

A few days later, at the end of February, Macmillan's aeroplane crashed during a night takeoff from Algiers, on his way to persuade a Vichy French admiral to hand over his fleet to the Allies. With flames all around him, his moustache on fire, he dragged himself out of the pilot's side window, landing hard on the ground. Just as he had done in the trenches in the First World War, he behaved with great bravery, rushing back into the plane to rescue another man still trapped there, before being was rushed to hospital, barely conscious and, apparently thinking he was back in the Somme in 1916, asking for a message to be sent to his mother, who had been dead for seven years. From hospital he wrote a chatty, witty letter to Eden, saying that he was happy to be out of the Commons: *The purely Balkan politics we have here are more to my liking. If you don't like a chap, you don't deprive him of the whip ... You just say he is a Monarchist, or has plotted to kill Murphy, and you shoot him off to prison or a Saharan concentration camp.*

*Then a week or two later, you let him out and make him Minister of something or other.*[6] After a week, heavily bandaged and temporarily bearded, though still in great pain and against his doctor's advice, he was boarding another plane to fulfil the mission he had had to abandon. He cultivated a sort of jokey insouciance about flying, once remarking as he looked down over the Sahara Desert: *So much bunker and not enough fairway*.

Saving General de Gaulle from himself still occupied many of his waking hours, and this frequently involved preventing the general from doing what he wanted to do, and telling him things he did not want to hear. He got little enough thanks from de Gaulle, but he knew that General Giraud – *so nice and also so stately and so stupid* – would not do: the war effort needed the brilliant, charismatic, difficult general instead. That meant keeping the two generals, for the time being, working together, and forcing de Gaulle to pledge publicly that he did not intend to try to establish a personal autocracy after France was liberated.

On 13 May the Axis forces in Tunisia surrendered. Macmillan the romantic had tears in his eyes as he stood beside General Eisenhower on the saluting base at the victory parade in Tunis. Macmillan the practical politician knew that he had to act fast, otherwise *Gaullists and Giraudists, now that there are no Germans to fight, will soon start a civil war amongst themselves*, and he flew to London just in time to stop the Prime Minister from abandoning de Gaulle. He assured Churchill that he could bring the two sides together. Against the odds, he did. Three weeks after the Axis surrender, the French Committee for National Liberation was formed, with de Gaulle and Giraud as joint presidents, and Macmillan was determined to get recognition for it from the British and the Americans. President Roosevelt still wanted to see Giraud as the leader, and, like many American presidents since then, failed to realise that showing obvious favour only harmed Giraud in the eyes of fellow Frenchmen. That, plus Giraud's ineptness, helped ensure that as the weeks went by, de Gaulle emerged as the FCNL's real leader. Macmillan, as one biographer puts it, 'had overcome the prejudices of the Americans, the irritation of London and the frequently impossible behaviour of de Gaulle himself'.[7]

Macmillan's services as de Gaulle's guardian angel were to be required once more before the war was done, when the French general's high-handed behaviour in the French mandates of Syria and the Lebanon almost caused Roosevelt and Churchill, not just to abandon him, but to destroy him. They would probably have done so, had Macmillan not, at his own request, been drafted back to construct one of his quick, clever compromises. But by then de Gaulle had become a sideshow in Macmillan's life. He had moved seamlessly on to the next theatre or war, Italy.

The Allies successfully invaded Sicily in 1943, Mussolini was overthrown, King Victor Emmanuel took control of his kingdom again with the aged Marshal Badoglio in charge of the government, and Macmillan and Murphy negotiated armistice terms with them. This was not made easy for them by their political masters, who wasted precious weeks arguing in London and Washington about what the terms should be, eventually producing a very long document which would have been humiliating for the Italians to sign. Macmillan had meanwhile produced a very short document, consisting of ten purely military conditions, which avoided the words 'unconditional surrender'. As the Germans were building up their forces south of Rome, Macmillan was able to tell his political masters that there was no more time to waste, and London should settle for his short document – which, grumbling, the Foreign Office agreed to do.

He moved to Allied headquarters at Caserta, where he stayed for the rest of the war, and watched the long Italian campaign as it devastated the countryside and the people. The day the armistice was signed, the Germans seized Rome, and Macmillan began to devote all the energy and political skill he had used on de Gaulle's behalf in support of the 73-year-old Italian king, who he thought would be a symbol of Italian national unity. This was not popular in London, where there was little love for Italian kings and politicians, nor among the generals on the spot, who felt military contempt for Italians. It was even less popular in Washington, which believed in governing Italy direct rather than letting Italians do it – the opposite of Macmillan's approach. But so long as Macmillan was at one with Murphy, Eisenhower listened to both of them, and Churchill listened to Macmillan, he would always have a chance.

**Mussolini** was deposed in July 1943, and placed under house arrest in the Appenine mountains, but was released in an airborne commando operation by the German Major Otto Skorzeny on 12 September. The Germans had been expecting the Italian surrender and had moved quickly to secure most of northern Italy under Operation Achse ('Axis'). Mussolini was set up as head of the puppet Italian Social Republic, known as the Salo Republic. In 1945 Mussolini was captured by partisans as he attempted to flee with his mistress. They were both shot and their bodies strung up in the streets of Milan.

But in 1944, the political requirements of Roosevelt's re-election campaign were all that American policy seriously considered, and Victor Emmanuel was not popular in New York's Italian community. Macmillan was privately angry that, when the Italians were starving and one in two newborn babies in Rome were dying, the Americans, instead of sending food, were trying to send New York politicians of

Italian origin – *to give good jobs to people strong in the New York Italian community*. He did manage to keep Victor Emmanuel's rule just about alive, only to see the Italians vote for a republic in June 1946.

Field Marshal Sir Harold Alexander, Macmillan's closest friend among the military commanders, wanted to march through Italy to Vienna. Macmillan flew to London and persuaded Churchill that it was the right strategy, but opposition from Eden and, crucially, the Americans ensured his defeat. Roosevelt was determined to stay with the plan agreed with Churchill at Casablanca, which meant that the invasion, when it came, would be through France, not through Italy; and which required the removal of many of the troops, as well as the supreme commander, Eisenhower, from Italy. Macmillan was always sure that a great opportunity had been lost. Had his plan been adopted, it *might have altered the whole political destinies of the Balkans and Eastern Europe*.

Foreign Secretary Anthony Eden was starting to get irritated with his old chum Harold Macmillan, who now wielded enormous influence and even power in the Mediterranean, was reporting direct to the Prime Minister instead of to him, and whose views on how to handle Italy had been at odds with those of the Foreign Office.

**Josip Broz Tito** (1892–1980) lead the Communist partisans in Yugoslavia during the Second World War, winning Allied support as the most effective resistance to the Germans, and took power in 1945. Tito's independence from Moscow allowed him to play off both East and West during the Cold War, and he came to head the so-called Non-Aligned Movement of Third World countries. Under Tito, Yugoslavia's ethnic tensions were contained, but after his death the Balkan wars of the 1990s soon followed. (See *Life&Times: Tito* by Neil Barnett.)

Eden now believed that Macmillan coveted his job. There was little he could do except grumble: to Eden's fury, Churchill made Macmillan Chief Commissioner of the Allied Control Commission, in effect the man who administered Italy. And not just Italy. He negotiated with Yugoslavian leader Marshal Tito, and took control of Greek politics as well. He was fast becoming the dominant British voice in the Mediterranean.

In Yugoslavia he backed the effective and popular Communists under Marshal Tito, and managed to defuse American fury. In Greece, he was tiptoeing into a quagmire. Churchill believed that the key to an anti-Communist Greece was the restoration of the monarchy, and committed British troops to fight the Greek partisans on the King's behalf. Macmillan thought Churchill was wrong: it meant fighting the people who had fought the Germans in order to put into power a reactionary and quasi-fascist government. And the position of the British troops was not at all good – it was by no means sure that they could take control of the country. Macmillan, after a dangerous sea voyage to Greece, was holed up and under siege in the embassy with fighting all around him, searching for a way through the morass, cabling London regularly that the King was an unpleasant autocrat not worth shedding British blood for, and edging towards the idea of appointing Archbishop Damaskinos as regent, to hold real power while the King became a sort of constitutional monarch – an idea which held no appeal at all for the King. Meanwhile the country lurched towards civil war,

Damaskinos had the respect in Greece which the King lacked, and Macmillan had taken to this splendid figure *– well over six foot – in black robes, with a black hood draped over his Orthodox hat, and a long black ebony cane with a silver top who intoned a blessing in a fine musical baritone ... dignified, traditional, and immensely impressive.*[8] Damaskinos returned his admiration, writing to him later: 'Your penetrating intelligence, your devotion to my country, and the friendship you have shown me since then, have been of invaluable assistance in the difficult path I have had to follow.'[9] But Churchill disliked the idea of Damaskinos, whom he denounced alternately as a Quisling and as a Communist, and announced that he was flying to Athens himself to sort out the mess. Eden had no intention of leaving Churchill and Macmillan to cook up a solution between them, and insisted on coming too. So the three men found themselves spending Christmas 1944 in a cold Athens to the sound of gunfire, where Macmillan sold Damaskinos to the Prime Minister, and the Foreign Secretary fumed.

Dreadful things happen in war, and war leaders sometimes make dreadful decisions which seem to them unavoidable. Macmillan's last big war decision seemed to him – and seems to us now – to be something like a war crime. Early in the war, 40,000 Cossacks and White Russians had taken up arms with the Germans. The Soviets wanted them back, and Macmillan had little doubt that if he handed them over, he was sending them to their deaths. There seemed no alternative – to refuse would rupture the alliance. Macmillan agreed.

Macmillan had had a good war. It made his career. But it did not seem so at the time. Back in London after VE Day, feted by those who mattered but virtually unknown in the country, he became for a few weeks Secretary of State for Air in Churchill's caretaker government after Labour withdrew from the coalition and a general election was called. He had an idea at least a fortnight before polling day of what would happen to him: 'Harold Macmillan ... thinks he has lost Stockton' wrote Cuthbert Headlam in his diary.[10] He was swept aside by the Labour landslide, and left wondering whether, at 51, his political career was over.

# Chapter 6: Attlee and Churchill remake Britain (1945–55)

By the end of 1945, Macmillan was back in Parliament, parachuted into the safe southern seat of Bromley as one of the men Churchill admired most, and appointed at once to the 14-strong Shadow Cabinet. In those days members of the Shadow Cabinet did not normally hold specific briefs, and he had plenty of scope to talk about anything he liked. What he chose to talk about, mostly, was economics, where he revelled in his freedom to say things which would have been heresy in the pre-war Conservative Party.

For the fact is that the Attlee settlement was something Macmillan approved of. He welcomed the creation of a welfare state along the lines foreshadowed in the Beveridge Report of 1942, to slay what Beveridge called the five giants of want, disease, ignorance, squalor and idleness, by the creation of a free National Health Service, child allowances and full employment. He did not even quarrel seriously with Labour's nationalisation measures. The post-war consensus built up over the six years of Attlee's government was bolstered by compassionate Conservatives like Macmillan, and lasted for 34 years until broken by Margaret Thatcher's 1979 election victory. His own side suspected that he was struggling to find something to quarrel with, as they listened to him speak acidly against, not nationalisation itself, but the remarkable rapidity of its implementation.

The truth was that Macmillan knew, perhaps faster than his colleagues, that the Conservative Party had to change with the times. The class-ridden society which his party represented was utterly out of tune with the spirit of the immediate post-war years. He, faster than other Conservatives, grasped the lesson of Labour's landslide victory at a time when the Conservatives were led by a national hero in the form of Winston Churchill. The voters were not rejecting Churchill; they were rejecting the Conservative Party of the 1930s, the years of mass unemployment and hunger marches, and welcomed a party which – to take just one example – made proper medical care available to the poor as it had always been available to the rich.

It was Macmillan, as much as anyone, who pressed for the wholesale policy review agreed by the October 1946 Conservative Party conference, which laid the foundations for his party's return to government in 1951. And it was Macmillan as much as anyone who inspired its direction – a direction he had already mapped out in *The Middle Way*. On one issue he was ahead of not only the Conservatives but the government as well, and that was Europe. He was one of the moving spirits of the 12-nation Council of Europe in 1949 and supported the creation of the six-nation Coal and Steel Community, which was eventually to become what we know as the European Union, yet as late as 1951 Attlee could say wearily to a group of young junior ministers: 'I want you to go to this new thing called the Council of Europe. I don't know much about it, but in your time, you'll have to.'[1]

But broadly he supported Labour foreign policy – hardly surprising since Foreign Secretary Ernest Bevin, the stout, pugnacious trade union leader whom Churchill had dragged out of impending retirement to serve as Minister of Labour during the war, was now pursuing a ferociously anti-Communist foreign policy that could have been mapped out by the Conservative Party. Listening to a Bevin speech, one Conservative MP remarked to his neighbour: 'Hasn't Anthony Eden got fat.' Personally Macmillan rather despised Bevin – and there was some of the old Macmillan snobbery in this, for Bevin was working-class and uneducated – but politically he found little to criticise, confiding in his diary when he heard of Bevin's death in 1951: *Bevin was in many ways a very bad Foreign Secretary. His Palestine policy was absurd, for he succeeded in the almost impossible result of becoming equally odious to Arab and Jew. His attitude to united Europe was petty. But he has done one immense service to Britain and the world. He has imposed on an unwilling and hesitant party a policy of resistance to Soviet Russia and to Communism. A Tory Foreign Secretary (in the immediate post-war years) could not have done this.*[2]

**Ernest Bevin** (1881–1951) was born in Somerset to poor parents, and was an orphan by the age of six. After a couple of years of formal education, Bevin became a farm labourer. At 18 he moved to Bristol where he found work as a van driver, joining the Dockers' Union and becoming one of its paid officials before he was 30. He was the key figure in the series of union mergers which created the giant Transport and General Workers Union, whose first general secretary he became in 1921, holding the post until 1940 when he joined Churchill's wartime coalition government as Minister of Labour and National Service. In 1945 Attlee made him Foreign Secretary, a job he held until a few months before his death.

The 1950 general election saw Labour returned but with a majority of only 18, and a further election in October 1951 at last returned Churchill to No 10 Downing Street. Macmillan hoped to be Minister of Defence, but Churchill appropriated that role for himself, as he had done during the war – a very foolish move, thought Macmillan, and so did many others with a less personal interest in the matter. It took a few days before Macmillan was summoned to Chartwell to see the Prime Minister, and the dreadful thought crossed his mind that he might get nothing.

*He asked me to 'build the houses for the people'*, wrote Macmillan in his diary. *What an assignment! I know nothing whatever about these matters, having spent 6 years now either on defence or foreign affairs ... Can we build 300,000 houses? That is what we are pledged to do ... Churchill says it is a gamble – make or mar my political career. But every humble home will bless my name, if I succeed. I said I would think about it ... On the whole it seems impossible to refuse – but, oh dear, it is not my cup of tea.*[3] In this mood he began the job that was soon to make him a man no Conservative leader could afford to ignore.

For his tenure was an unexpected and startling success-story. For three years he dedicated himself to the achievement of the 300,000 target, which his civil servants told him was unachievable. The department had languished since it lost the dynamic Aneurin Bevan, who in the immediate post-war years had combined housing with health, and Macmillan restructured it and infected it with new dynamism, determined to allow nothing to stand between him and the achievement of the target. He forced the Cabinet to agree the economic stringency they applied to everything else should not apply to anything he needed for housebuilding, and the Cabinet let him get away with it, partly because he presented his case skilfully, partly because he had the Prime Minister's support, but mainly, no doubt, because he was in charge of delivering the Conservatives' only measurable pledge. He also reduced still further the standards of the houses built. The best and most spacious council houses were those built by Bevan in the late 1940s, and it was these which were sold off first when Margaret Thatcher's government started selling council houses. The standards were lowered by Bevan's Labour successors, and then lowered again by Macmillan. And in 1954 he was able to boast the achievement of the target.

That year he had his reward – the Ministry of Defence, which is what he wanted in the first place. He soon found that he had been better off at housing. Churchill could leave his housing minister to get on with the job, but not his defence minister, who found the Prime Minister wanting to have his fingers in every pie. The three service ministers were very powerful, and it was hard to find an area in which he might have real control. Churchill and Eden did not share his enthusiasm for Europe, and he was not allowed to join the European Defence Community nor to strengthen the influence of the Council of Europe. The shortsightedness of Labour's attitude towards Europe was being exactly replicated by the Conservatives, to the distress of the new defence minister. Fortunately for Macmillan, his stay in defence lasted only six months. Churchill resigned on 5 April 1955, and Eden, the heir-apparent for many years, became Prime Minister. Now Macmillan was to get the job he wanted most in politics: Foreign Secretary.

It worried him little that he was Eden's second choice. The Prime Minister would far rather have had his old friend, and Macmillan's contemporary and brother-in-law, Lord Salisbury, but was persuaded that the Foreign Secretary could not be in the House of Lords. (This did not trouble Macmillan two years later when he gave Lord Home the job.) Whatever the reason, it had a wider significance than was obvious at the time, for Macmillan represented the new Conservatism, heavily influenced by his 1930s pamphlet *The*

*Middle Way*, whereas increasingly Lord Salisbury reflected the sort of conservatism which looked back to the party's great days.

It was the summit of Macmillan's ambition. He thought then, as he said many years later, that *if Anthony's government lasts five years, I'll be 65 or so and I will have had five years at the Foreign Office. Then I shall retire. That will be enough.*[4] He wrote a caption to a picture of himself in the Foreign Secretary's chair: *I had often dreamed of sitting in this room, and I finally realised it in 1955*. Given that he was over 60 and older than his Prime Minister, this seemed the limit of his realistic expectations too. The family political banner would then be carried by Maurice, who entered Parliament at that election. But he added: *My tenure of the Foreign Office was all too brief before Anthony Eden, one of our greatest Foreign Secretaries, moved me on to the Treasury.*[5]

*If Anthony's government lasts five years, I'll be 65 or so and I will have had five years at the Foreign Office. Then I shall retire. That will be enough.*

MACMILLAN

That was a diplomatic way of complaining that his tenure was not only brief, but frustrating. Just as Churchill could not stay out of defence, so Eden could not stay out of foreign affairs. According to Macmillan, Eden was constantly telephoning and sending him notes, sometimes 20 a day. Eden certainly did not want in the job an increasingly influential politician with his own mind and the weight that comes from experience of international affairs.

'It was,' writes the Conservative historian John Charmley, 'a sign of the lack or confidence which was eventually to undermine him that Eden did not feel able to appoint his old friend and supporter Lord Salisbury to the post of Foreign Secretary; and it was a symptom of his fidgetiness that, having appointed Macmillan to it, he wanted to move him as soon as the election was over.'[6]

1955 had provided not only a new Prime Minister but also a new Leader of the Opposition. The old Prime Minister and opposition leader, Winston Churchill and Clement Attlee, were the men who had fought the war. Their replacements were the first major party leaders not closely associated with the politics of the 1930s. Even though Anthony Eden had joined the Cabinet at the end of the 1930s, it was late in the decade and the issue had become war, not poverty; and the new Labour leader, Hugh Gaitskell, was a politician of the new post-war generation, who had entered Parliament in 1945.

**Nikita Khrushchev** (1894–1971) became First Secretary of the Communist Party in 1953. Beginning as a reformist, he denounced Stalin's cult of personality in the 'Secret Speech' of 1956 and became Premier in 1958. Although there was some liberalisation and economic growth at home, Khrushchev also ordered the invasion of Hungary in 1956, encouraged the building of the Berlin Wall and stationed Soviet missiles in Cuba, which brought the world to the brink of nuclear war. He was deposed in 1964, and spent the remaining seven years of his life under house arrest.

Macmillan's old wartime friendship with Eisenhower was an advantage, of course, as was his knack of making light of things. When US Secretary of State Foster Dulles suggested that the US might be represented at a heads of state meeting by the Vice President, Richard Nixon, Macmillan recalled in his memoirs: *Thinking this was a joke, I told him of the famous music hall joke: 'Poor Mrs Jones, what a terrible thing has happened to her ... She had two fine sons. One of them went down in the Titanic, the other became vice president of the United States. Neither of them was ever heard of again ...'*[7] Dulles took the hint and the President came himself. He brought to the job, not just the Macmillan wit, but the arriviste snobbery, which was affronted by his first meeting with Nikita Khrushchev. *How can this fat, vulgar man, with his pig eyes and ceaseless flow of talk, really be the head – the aspirant Tsar – of all these millions of people and this vast country?*[8]

But what Eden really wanted was a cipher. He did not want to be his own Foreign Secretary, as Ramsay MacDonald had been, but he did want to run foreign policy. He needed a cipher, and found one in the hardworking but uninspiring lawyer Selwyn Lloyd, who hardly ever went abroad, did not think much of foreigners, and knew little of foreign affairs. Macmillan was by now far too powerful a figure to be fired or demoted, but not too powerful to be shifted, against his will, to the Exchequer. Rab Butler badly wanted a break. He had been Chancellor for four difficult years, he had faced massive criticism for his last budget, and his wife had died of cancer the previous December, leaving him unhappy and listless. But Macmillan never believed that this was Eden's real reason for moving him to the Exchequer, and the appointment of Selwyn Lloyd suggests he was right.

Macmillan drove as hard a bargain as he could, and his growing stature in the Party gave him some leverage. He extracted promises of autonomy, he blocked the proposal to make Butler deputy Prime Minister, he delayed, but in the end he went to the Exchequer, which is where he was when the earthquake we know as Suez hit the government.

# Chapter 7: 'Wab or Hawold?' (1956)

Did Macmillan or any other minister realise how momentous a year 1956 was to prove? Macmillan may have foreseen a small part of it: he noted in his diary for 28 December 1955: *Randolph* [Churchill] *(who hates Anthony and calls him 'jerk') prophesies an early collapse of the govt …* Two days later, sitting at his Treasury desk, he noted that his predecessor Rab Butler had left the finances in a poor state, and he feared *total collapse, under Harold Macmillan*!

His hopes for the year included a heartfelt personal one. All the four Macmillan children suffered from the Devonshire disease of alcoholism, and the oldest, Maurice, was in a very bad state. On 16 January Maurice was to leave for a cure in Switzerland, and the dinner with him the previous night was, wrote Macmillan, *rather melancholy … He is in a thoroughly bad state of health and must try to get put right now*. He was there for six months, returning in late July looking well. But it did not last.

Meanwhile British industry was in the doldrums. Costs and wages were rising fast, but productivity was not. Macmillan's first thoughts would have been heresy for a Conservative Chancellor two decades earlier, including as they did raising income tax and slashing defence spending. The latter had been part of his thinking when he was Foreign Secretary. *It has now become quite clear*, he wrote to Butler in August

1955, *that there is really no protection against a nuclear attack, certainly in these islands. The only protection is the deterrent of a counter attack. What then is the purpose of spending these immense sums* [on conventional defences]*?* As Chancellor he told Eden in April the next year: *It is defence expenditure which has broken our backs*. Unless he cut it, he would have to put up taxes sharply. Eden would not allow either, but Macmillan went on demanding them. *I feel I must tell you*, he wrote to Eden after his budget, *how anxious I am about the state of the economy. We are like a man in the early stages of consumption, flushed cheek and apparent health concealing the disease ...*[1] A threat of resignation got him much of what he wanted. He was pleased that what was a real Cabinet crisis was kept entirely secret: not a word leaked into the newspapers. *The whole country seems – perhaps fortunately – more interested in the Death Penalty than in economics*. Secrecy is something the Eden government was rather good at – a talent that was to prove its downfall. Macmillan also launched Premium Bonds as a way to encourage saving and raise revenue.

Introduced as 'Savings with a thrill', Premium Bonds offered no interest, but each bond was entered in a monthly prize draw (a maximum £500 of bonds could be held), the original maximum prize being £1,000, and bonds could be cashed in at cost at any time. By the time of the first prize draw in June 1957, bonds worth £82 million had been bought. In the 50 years of their existence, prizes worth £8.5 billion have been paid out, and the current value of bonds held is £30 billion.

The trade unions, in those days a real force in the land, seemed to be putty in the Chancellor's patrician hands. Just as the aristocratic Devonshires had once laughed at the way he turned up overdressed for the grouse moors, so now Macmillan confided with amusement to his diary that the horny-handed sons of toil *all behaved beautifully and were so respectable, with their dark blue suits and bowlers, that they looked like a lot of undertakers*. He *distributed various 'secret' documents to them – which they seemed to like.*[2] He sent them away happy, presumably patting them kindly on their heads and giving them each a shiny new sixpence.

He still watched foreign affairs with close interest, worrying especially about the Middle East. Britain's 1936 treaty with Egypt required the removal of British troops from the Suez Canal by 1956. But in 1952, the Egyptian king was deposed, and the country's new leader was General Neguib, who was himself ousted two years later by Colonel Gamal Abdel Nasser. This seemed to the British press – and to Eden and Macmillan – to be a bad development, for Nasser wanted to radically reduce his country's reliance on the West – even to the extent of buying his arms from the Soviet Union. *If we lose out in the M.East, we lose the oil. If we lose the oil, we cannot live*, Macmillan wrote in his diary on 12 January.

*If we lose out in the M.East, we lose the oil. If we lose the oil, we cannot live.*
MACMILLAN

On 16 March Macmillan wrote in his diary: *Some rather alarming news is reaching us about Nasser. He seems to be aiming at a sort of League of Arab Republics (the monarchies are to go) to include Libya, Tunisia, Algeria, Morocco as well as the Arab states in Asia Minor etc. Egypt wd have a sort of hegemony in this League, wh wd be a strong and immensely rich affair, esp if the oil resources were pooled. To start it off, and gain prestige, Egypt will attack Israel in June (after the last British soldiers have left Egypt under the Treaty). They will seize a part of Israel's territory (Beersheba area) and when called on to stop by the United Nations, they will do so. But they will not retreat and hold on to their gain, and establish tremendous popularity etc with all Arabs. Of course this plan (knowledge of which comes from fairly good sources and sounds quite plausible) has one defect. If the Egyptians attack the Jews, they will prob (in spite of their superiority in weapons) get a bloody nose. They may even have a shattering defeat, which would tumble Nasser off his perch.* It is a remarkably revealing passage, far more so than its author intended. This convoluted plot which Macmillan was attributing (probably wrongly) to the malignity of Nasser was almost the same as the plot Eden eventually entered into with the French and the Israelis.

But there is little evidence that, in March, he thought of Suez as much more than a sideshow. In foreign affairs, it was Greece and Cyprus which occupied most of his attention, and both were entirely overshadowed by the looming economic crisis. If he thought it was a bad summer, it was because problems were piling up. On 5 July they had *a three hours cabinet … – every question gets more difficult. Cyprus, Ceylon, Middle East: then hanging; a steel strike; the motor car situation* [there was to be a strike at the British Motor Corporation] *etc.* A couple of weeks later, on 21 July, *nothing has gone very well. In the M East we are still being teased by Nasser and Co; the Colonial Empire is breaking up …* . On top of it all, the Prime Minister's colleagues started to see that he was in decline, both politically and in terms of his always fragile health.

**Gamal Abdel Nasser** (1918–70) was one of the army officers who staged a coup in Egypt in 1952. Becoming President in 1956, his defiance of the former colonial powers over the Suez Canal won him widespread popularity in the Arab world. In 1958 he formed the United Arab Republic with Syria, but this collapsed three years later. Defeat by Israel in the Six-Day War of 1967 was a major blow, leading to his temporary resignation. He died of a heart attack in 1970. (See *Life & Times: Nasser* by Anne Alexander.)

On 27 July Nasser nationalised the Suez Canal Company. Macmillan's diary note was: *Nasser has declared his intention to 'nationalise' – that is, seize, the Suez Canal Company* ... Nasser had said he would use the Canal revenue to pay for the building of the Aswan Dam, since the British and Americans had withdrawn their offer of funding. Macmillan thought Nasser *an Asiatic Mussolini* and wrote: *The unanimous view of the Cabinet was in favour of strong and resolute action*. Eden appointed an 'Egypt Committee' – himself, Salisbury, Lord Home and Macmillan. It became the real power in the Suez crisis, bypassing the Cabinet.

It did not escape old campaigners like Eden and Macmillan that 1956 was the 20th anniversary of Hitler's occupation of the Rhineland – indeed it could be said that they were mesmerised by the shadow of the *Führer*. They also knew that Britain was the largest single Canal user as well as the biggest single shareholder in the Suez Canal Company. But by 30 July it was, wrote Macmillan, *clear that the Americans are going to 'restrain' us all they can*. Britain gave the American diplomat Bob Murphy the impression that the fleet was ready to sail (though it would take at least six weeks). By the next day *it seems that we have succeeded in thoroughly alarming Murphy* and Secretary of State John Foster Dulles was coming over himself. *This is a very good development*, wrote Macmillan in his diary.

With a Foreign Secretary who knew he was not suited to the job, and was being used as a cipher by a sick, tense and overstretched Prime Minister, Macmillan was emerging as the government's chief Suez strategist. Ministers' thoughts were focused on the USA. On 1 August Macmillan saw Dulles. *I told Foster, as plainly as I could, that we just could not afford to lose this game. It was a question not*

*I told Foster, as plainly as I could, that we just could not afford to lose this game. It was a question not of honour but of survival.*

MACMILLAN

*of honour but of survival. We must either get Nasser out by diplomacy or by force ... I think he was quite alarmed; for he had hoped to find me less extreme, I think. We must keep the Americans really frightened ... Then they will help us to get what we want, without the necessity for force. But we must have a) international control of the Canal b) humiliation and collapse of Nasser ...*

Strangely for a man with such good American contacts and such sensitive political antennae, he completely misunderstood the Americans. On 19 August, when Dulles would not implement new economic sanctions, he wrote: *I cannot help feeling that* [Dulles] *really wants us to 'go it alone' and is trying to help us by creating the right atmosphere ...* This was an extraordinarily perverse interpretation of the legalistic Dulles's clear unhappiness about Britain's Egypt policy.

August saw plans for invasion being assessed and discussed. Macmillan found money for war preparations despite the economic crisis. He mourned the loss of wartime censorship powers which would have prevented the newspapers from printing details of troop movements, and predicted they would need them again. He pressed the Admiralty for powers to requisition liners. He wanted a full agreement with the French about an invasion, and became more convinced of the need to bring in Israel *otherwise it couldn't be done*. He swapped notes with Churchill, which made Eden very angry and jealous, thinking Macmillan was conspiring with Churchill against him. He had no sympathy with the anti-war papers and politicians, writing rather Blimpishly on 8 August, *It's the Liberal intellectual who is always against his country*.

But by early September he was starting to appreciate that the position was grim. The Americans were wobbling, negotiations with Nasser were making no headway, and the press started to accuse Eden of making plans for war behind the backs of the people. Military chiefs were warning that

Egypt, with its Soviet and Czech weapons, was not a negligible military force. Egypt had also shown that it did not intend to close the Canal, and that Egyptian pilots were quite capable of guiding ships through it, so removing part of the excuse for attacking the country. There were increasing expert doubts about the legality of using force against Egypt. And Eisenhower had to face re-election in November. It seems extraordinary that no one in the British government seems to have wondered whether he really wanted an international crisis a day or two before polling day.

The Labour Party was now firmly opposed to war. So were the Liberals, and so was the Archbishop of Canterbury, which *put us in a difficult position, esp as a good many Tories, mostly young and mostly sons of Munichites – like Richard Wood – began to rat too.* This sort of illogical bitterness is not like Macmillan, and is a measure of how far his normally excellent judgement deserted him that summer, during which he successfully resisted the idea that Britain might pledge not to use force without UN agreement. His contempt for his one-time friend Robert Boothby knew no bounds: *Boothby, characteristically, made a fighting speech yesterday and was in full retreat today.* Britain's position was crumbling, but none of those in charge of British policy seem to have realised it.

Eden was preoccupied with his neurotic worry that his Chancellor had strayed too far beyond his economic brief, and keeping him out of many major decisions. But Macmillan, whether intentionally or not, put himself at centre stage with a long-planned visit to Washington at the end of September, to attend a meeting of the International Monetary Fund. This visit, as it turns out, was crucial to everything that followed. As an old wartime friend and colleague of President Eisenhower, he had the rare privilege of a private audience in the Oval Office. Eisenhower was very cordial. *It was just like talking to him in the old days at the St George's Hotel in Algiers.* They reminisced about old times, and talked a little about Suez. Macmillan also met Dulles, who seems to have said that he wanted peace to be kept until the presidential election on 6 November – and emphasised this point by reminding Macmillan that the Americans had helped the Tories at the general election the previous year. Somehow, Macmillan managed to come away firmly convinced that the Americans would support military action over Suez, and encouraged his Prime Minister's natural propensity to believe the same thing. Roger Makins, Ambassador in Washington, was present at the meeting with Eisenhower, and he said later that there was no basis for Macmillan's optimism.

Almost as soon as he returned from the USA, Macmillan's diary ceases to exist, and there are no entries from 4 October until 3 February. Macmillan claimed at first to have lost them, then admitted to destroying them at Eden's request. Quite what happened, we cannot be sure, but from what we do know, it does not look as though either Eden or Macmillan did much in the next few months that they could later be proud of. For it was now that they hatched the curious, hare-brained and dishonest Israel plot. As long ago as August, Macmillan had been quietly musing that bringing Israel into the crisis might have its advantages, but now a real chance seemed to present itself. Meetings were held at which secretaries were asked to withdraw, or to take no minutes, or whose minutes were destroyed.

The plot was this. Israel would attack Egypt across Sinai. Britain and France would call on both sides to withdraw from the Canal. Nasser was sure to refuse, and this would enable Britain and France to place their armies, supposedly as a peacemaking force, between the Egyptian and Israeli forces – and take control of the Canal and humiliate Nasser. Thus it was, at the height of President Eisenhower's whistle-stop campaign for re-election, on 27 October, with just ten days to go before polling day, that he heard of Israel's full-scale mobilisation, and sent a telegram to Prime Minister Ben Gurion urging him to 'do nothing to endanger the peace'. Israel invaded Sinai two days later.

Events moved fast. The next day Britain and France issued their ultimatum to Israel and Egypt. Israel accepted it, but advanced nonetheless – and an eager young colonel called Ariel Sharon exceeded his orders, taking all his objectives at once. No one had explained to Colonel Sharon that he was depriving Britain and France of their flimsy excuse to invade, by completing his mission and ensuring there was no further fighting which the European powers could step in and put a stop to.

Egypt, of course, rejected the Anglo-French ultimatum. On 31 October Britain started bombing Egyptian airfields and defence installations, and a fleet sailed from Malta. In the House of Commons, Selwyn Lloyd explicitly denied any prior agreement with Israel. He lied. So did Eden. 'I asked Eden, I think it was his last appearance in the House of Commons, whether we had any foreknowledge of the Israeli attack and he told a straight lie', recalled the Labour MP Denis Healey. Eden and Macmillan gave every appearance of being delighted with themselves. But opinion polls showed British public opinion was against them, although much of the press was busy building up a jingoistic (and racist) campaign against the Egyptians. They clearly thought they could ride the opposition of their voters, but then came opposition which Macmillan knew at once he could not ride.

Six days before polling day in the presidential election, without telling him, his old Conservative friends in Britain had thrown sand in President Eisenhower's face, and his wrath was terrible. He was concerned about the image of the US in the Arab world. And he had stood as the President for peace. It is very hard to see just how Eden and Macmillan failed to predict this – especially since it must now be clear to the President that his old British friends had been lying to him for weeks.

For the first time ever, the USA combined with the Soviet Union at the United Nations to condemn Britain and France. This must have been a bitter pill for Eisenhower to swallow, for in Eastern Europe, Hungary was in revolt against Soviet rule, and Eisenhower had hoped briefly to see Hungary break loose from behind the Iron Curtain. Yet now, at the worst possible moment, he needed Soviet support. Two days later, on 4 November, Soviet tanks entered Hungary. Eisenhower blamed the bumbling British for this disaster too, and with some justice, for it was part of the Soviet rulers' calculation that the West was too distracted by Suez to oppose them effectively. And there were two days to go to polling day. It is not hard to see why those close to the President reported that whenever he could get away from the campaign trail and be private, he filled the air with 'barrack room language' about the British government.

**Dwight D Eisenhower** (1890–1969) was Supreme Allied Commander in Europe from 1944 until the end of the Second World War, organising the D-Day landings and the defeat of Nazi Germany in the West. In 1951 he returned to Europe as Supreme Commander of NATO, but was persuaded to run as Republican presidential candidate in 1952, easily defeating the Democrat Stevenson to become the first soldier-president since Grant. His presidency saw a heightening of Cold War tensions and anti-Communist fears. He was re-elected in 1956, and retired in 1961 after warning of the growth of the 'military-industrial complex'.

The British landings went ahead on 5 November. The next day Eisenhower won his expected landslide victory. And straight away, Chancellor of the Exchequer Harold Macmillan reported to the Cabinet a serious run on the pound, orchestrated deliberately in Washington. Britain's gold reserves had fallen by an eighth, and only a ceasefire by midnight would bring American support for an IMF loan to prop up the pound. The IMF would not even allow Britain to withdraw her own money until it had begun its withdrawal from Suez. Eden's troops may have been in Nasser's backyard, but Eisenhower's tanks were on Eden's lawn. The Chancellor, who had spent months plotting to get Britain into Suez, told the Cabinet the day after they had landed that they must come out at once. Harold Wilson's jibe that Macmillan had been 'first in, first out' of Suez was wounding because it was absolutely true. Nasser's victory was complete. Egypt kept full ownership of the Suez Canal, and got Soviet support for the construction of the Aswan Dam, which was completed 14 years later. He was an instant hero in the Arab world.

It was as gross a miscalculation as any British government has made. *We altogether failed*, said Macmillan later, *to appreciate the force of the resentment which would be directed against us. For this I carry a heavy responsibility. I knew Eisenhower well ... and thought I understood his character ... I believed the Americans would issue a protest ... in public; but that they would in their hearts be glad to see the matter brought to a conclusion.*[3]

*We altogether failed to appreciate the force of the resentment which would be directed against us.*

MACMILLAN

It is extraordinary that two men with the experience and sophistication of Eden and Macmillan could have made such a miscalculation. Macmillan was an old and trusted friend of Eisenhower and Eden was one of the world's elder statesmen of international diplomacy. Macmillan was Chancellor, and knew the vulnerability of his economy.

Between them they ensured that, for at least the next half-century, no British government would act in any international matter of the slightest importance without first obtaining American permission; and that if the American government required action from a British government, it got that action. The one notable act of defiance throughout the next half-century was that Harold Wilson kept Britain out of Vietnam, a stand which was neither understood nor forgiven in Washington, where Wilson was frequently reminded that his was not a wealthy country, and could be bankrupted at will by the USA. Almost 50 years later, a new British Prime Minister, Tony Blair, sent British troops into Iraq in many of the same circumstances: the attack undermined the standing of the United Nations and was deeply unpopular with the British people. But this time, the Americans wanted it, and there was never any question of Blair being forced to bring his troops home.

Eden's health, always fragile, was now a cause of serious concern, and his doctors insisted on a complete rest. He flew to Jamaica on 23 November. Rab Butler, though Macmillan had successfully prevented him from being called Deputy Prime Minister, became acting PM. It fell to Butler, therefore, to handle the fallout of a policy towards which, certainly compared with Eden and Macmillan, he had always been lukewarm: to oversee the humiliating withdrawal, and to fend off attacks from press and Parliament, until Eden returned on 14 December. But Eden was not cured, his fevers returned, and just three weeks later, on 8 January 1957, he resigned.

Eden's health saved Britain from an even greater humiliation than those already loaded upon her. For the fact is that, even if he had been healthy, he would have had to go, since he no longer had the trust of the US government. Macmillan, and most of the Cabinet, knew Eden would have to go even before they knew that his health would force him to go. Because Eden was able to say, truthfully, that his health did not permit him to go on, the abject lesson from Suez did not have to be spelled out: that no British Prime Minister or Foreign Secretary can last if he or she loses the confidence of the US administration. Even though this is not normally put into words, every Prime Minister since then has shown by their behaviour that he was aware of it, starting with Macmillan and ending, at the time of writing, with Tony Blair – not a Prime Minister with a great sense of history, but one who has clearly learned that lesson. Even before the Iraq war, Blair unexpectedly fired a competent Foreign Secretary, Robin Cook, who was popular everywhere except in George W Bush's White House.

And it must have been one of the factors in the minds of the members of the Cabinet as they were called, one by one, into the room used by Conservative Party elder statesman (and Macmillan's old Eton friend, contemporary and brother-in-law) Lord Salisbury. Salisbury, who had the aristocratic inability to pronounce the letter R, asked each of them in turn: 'Well, which is it to be, Wab or Hawold?'[4] And pretty soon it was clear that the answer was going to be: Hawold.

*'Well, which is it to be, Wab or Hawold?'*

LORD SALISBURY

And that, on the face of it, is a little odd, for if anyone could be said to share the blame for the disaster almost equally with Eden, it was Macmillan. Butler's ambivalence had not won him friends in the Cabinet or the Conservative Party. Macmillan, despite Suez, seemed to be a safe pair of hands, as well as an officer and a gentleman. Butler seemed, in those frenetic days, to be none of those things.

Salisbury could not know, when he advised the Queen to send for Macmillan, that it marked the beginning of the end of his own political career, which had once seemed far more hopeful than that of his brother-in-law. He found that the man he had patronised for so many years was not much interested in his advice on Cabinet-forming, and was, before he was done, to embark on the dismantling of the Empire.

# Part Two

## THE LEADERSHIP

# Chapter 8: Plucking Victory from the Jaws of Defeat (1957–9)

The whole of the decade 1955–65 is really the Macmillan years. For though he only became Prime Minister in 1957, and resigned in 1963, he was, as Robert Blake puts it, 'the dominant figure in the cabinet under Eden and he virtually nominated his successor, Lord Home'.[1] Yet when he became Prime Minister, at the start of 1957, nothing could have seemed less likely than that he would seem to history to be one of our more significant Prime Ministers. He told the Queen that he might not last six weeks. She reminded him of this, six years later.

At home, the economy, which had been in deep trouble even before Suez, was in a state of near-collapse. Abroad, there was nothing but humiliation. The government had to reach some accommodation with the man it had wanted to destroy, Nasser, otherwise he could refuse to allow Britain's ships and oil through the Suez Canal. It had to find the least humiliating way of getting back into the good books of the US government. Under Attlee, Churchill and Eden, Britain had stayed aloof from the discussions which were soon to lead to the creation of a European Common Market, so without US patronage, there was nowhere in the world to hide.

And that is to ignore the scars of Suez on the national psyche. It is at least arguable that the rebellious 1960s really started with the Suez debacle, but no one noticed until 1964, when the nation elected the first Prime Minister who had not been a Second World War political leader, Harold Wilson. It was Suez which forced Britons to face the fact that their country no longer counted for much in the world, and the jingoism on which they had lived for the first half of the century was now a shallow farce. Even today, a person's attitude to patriotism and Britishness is partly dictated by whether they reached adulthood before Suez or after it. I was 11 in 1956 and cannot say the word 'patriotism' with a straight face. But a person only five years older than me can use the word entirely naturally.

> **Richard Austin ('Rab') Butler** (1902–82) was Minister of Education in the wartime government and was Chancellor from 1951 to 1955. Always seen as a future Prime Minister, and standing in for Churchill during his illnesses in the 1950s, he never achieved the top job, losing out to Macmillan in 1957 and to Douglas-Home in 1963. He retired from the Commons in 1965, having been Father of the House (the longest-serving member), and went to the House of Lords as Baron Butler of Saffron Walden, after the seat he had represented since 1929.

All Macmillan had on his side was time. He had a sizeable parliamentary majority, and Conservative MPs were not going to bring down the government and precipitate a general election at a moment when they were likely to lose it badly, and many of them to lose their seats. Macmillan had until 1960. The first job was putting together a government. Macmillan believed that *Butler (whose feelings of disappointment I could imagine only too well) was the key figure.*[2] He offered Butler any post he liked except Foreign Secretary. Eden's departure was bound to be seen abroad as a sacrifice to the Americans, and Macmillan did not want it to look as though Selwyn Lloyd was to be a second sacrifice. Perhaps also, like Eden, he wanted to be the real power in foreign policy. Butler took the Home Office.

Macmillan's old friend Salisbury, who had held the ring which gave him the premiership, agreed to stay on as Leader of the House of Lords, but quickly found his wings clipped. The ageing and increasingly reactionary peer, who had patronised Macmillan at Eton and in the Conservative Party and who, 30 years earlier, had wondered darkly whether this parvenu harboured treasonable thoughts about the sanctity of the British Empire, found within days of Macmillan's premiership that they were on the road that led the two men to bitter enmity. As Simon Ball writes: 'Salisbury was left in his room hoping that, although Macmillan was now the first among equals, he himself would retain a position of power, honour and influence. Only Macmillan knew that Salisbury would soon be powerless ... Salisbury would never again be consulted on an issue of political importance.'[3]

The break came fast. In Cyprus, Archbishop Makarios, leader of the Greek Cypriot nationalist movement, was in exile in the Seychelles. His followers were demanding him back, and the armed wing of the nationalist movement, EOKA, announced that they would stop attacking British forces there if they got him. This was not the time for a British government to be stiff-necked. Macmillan agreed. Salisbury, the old imperialist, was aghast. He had threatened resignation many times before in order to get his way, and it had worked. He believed that for a Conservative government to incur the undying wrath of the scion of the Cecils was unthinkable, and for many years it was. But time had moved on. Macmillan knew it, and Salisbury did not. The Prime Minister calmly accepted Salisbury's resignation. Not a lot of people knew that.

The tricky business of remaking the government with a splintered party took ten days, and was wearing and difficult. Macmillan handled it in the way that would become his trademark. He took plenty of time to sit and read: Trollope, Henry James, Cobbett's *Rural Rides*, Robert Louis Stevenson. He never allowed his mind to be taken over by politics, and never dwelt on his mistakes, the worst of which – Suez – it was now his job to put behind him. Later Prime Ministers might have done well to follow this example. Harold Wilson never switched off, and Macmillan once said of Margaret Thatcher: *I wish she would read a book.*

Having made his government, Macmillan's next priority was to revive the Anglo-American relationship. A great realist, he wasted no time on recrimination. His advantages were his wartime friendship with the President, and a letter Churchill had written to Eisenhower: 'There is not much left for me to do in this world and I have neither the wish nor the strength to involve myself in the present political stress and turmoil. But I do believe, with unfaltering conviction, that the theme of Anglo-American alliance is more important today than at any time since the war ...'[4] Apart from the fact that it came from a man Eisenhower admired, it was also a reminder that Eisenhower believed that too.

Within weeks, Macmillan was on a plane to Bermuda to meet Eisenhower. Personally, it was all friendly enough, but Britain's status as supplicant was never in doubt. Eisenhower offered to supply Britain with an American ballistic missile, equipped with nuclear warheads. To be any use against the Soviet Union, this would have to be based in Britain, so the offer was not exactly disinterested. Macmillan agreed. Secretly, they also agreed to refuse France any help in creating its own nuclear programme.

Macmillan appealed for help in getting a face-saving

agreement with Nasser which *we can claim as reasonable, if not quite what we would like ... I hope you will denounce Nasser and all his works ...* [5] He wanted fees for using the Canal paid to an international body, not to the Egyptian government. But he found the President unsympathetic, and was left to do the best he could with Nasser. He eventually settled the matter, on Nasser's terms, to French fury. The French wanted to boycott the Canal. French politicians were becoming surer by the moment that Britain had decided to put US friendship above European unity. This was to have serious long-term consequences for Macmillan's government. Potentially more immediately dangerous than French fury was that of right-wing Conservatives. Salisbury was especially incandescent. But Macmillan carried the House of Commons on the Suez deal, his able Chief Whip Edward Heath managing to reduce the number of abstentions to a manageable 14.

With foreign difficulties contained or neutralised, at least for the moment, Macmillan turned to the question of winning the next election. That task was made easier by Labour's disarray, for the split between Labour leader Hugh Gaitskell and the left, led by Aneurin Bevan, was at its height. But the great realist knew that, most of the time, foreign affairs neither win nor lose elections. *I am always hearing about the Middle Classes*, he wrote to the head of the Conservative research department. *What is it they really want? Can you put it down on a sheet of notepaper, and I will see if we can give it to them?*[6] That is pure Macmillan: the self-mocking lordliness, the apparently effortless superiority, combined with ruthless appreciation of the political reality that to win the election, he needed the middle classes.

*I am always hearing about the Middle Classes. What is it they really want?*
MACMILLAN

He recognised, too, the political reality memorably (if

less elegantly) encapsulated years later by Bill Clinton: 'It's the economy, stupid.' For the vital post of Chancellor of the Exchequer, Macmillan chose Peter Thorneycroft, who had been President of the Board of Trade under Churchill and Eden. Eight months into Thorneycroft's tenure, a sudden sterling crisis brought a run on the pound. No one, including Thorneycroft's Treasury advisers, had predicted it. It seems to have been caused by rumours of a devaluation, following the weakening of the pound after Suez and the devaluation of the French franc. But Thorneycroft's cerebral financial secretary, Enoch Powell, convinced him that the real problem was inflation, and the solution was to control the money supply and keep wage settlements down. Powell, an early Thatcherite with an almost religious devotion to the free market, turned Thorneycroft into what we would now call a monetarist – but it went against all the Prime Minister's instincts, and he asked his own favourite economist, Roy Harrod, the biographer of John Maynard Keynes, who told him: 'The idea that you can reduce prices by limiting the quantity of money is pre-Keynesian. Hardly any economist under the age of 50 subscribes to it.'[7]

For a while, Thorneycroft had his way, even though his Labour shadow Harold Wilson mounted effective Commons attacks on his measures, which included sharp bank rate rises and cuts in public spending. But these did not have the impact he expected, and he urged yet sharper cuts, including deep cuts in welfare spending, abolishing children's allowances and family allowances, and higher prescription charges. It was against all Macmillan's instincts. Thorneycroft threatened resignation. He should have learned from the fate of Lord Salisbury. Macmillan gave every indication of trying to find an accommodation with his Chancellor, even at one point telling the Cabinet that the whole government might have to resign. Thorneycroft resigned on 8 January 1959, Powell and economic secretary Nigel Birch going with him. Thorneycroft's resignation statement, according to Macmillan, was *calculated ... to do the maximum injury to Sterling. It sought to give the impression that he alone in the Cabinet stood out against inflation.*[8]

Thorneycroft had underestimated his Prime Minister. So did Powell, who became much better known in subsequent years, but never got over his loathing for Macmillan. Though both Butler and Macmillan were duplicitous, he wrote, 'there is in Mr Butler an ultimate sub-stratum of faith in things which I myself believe in'.[9] Years later, defending Margaret Thatcher, he wrote that Macmillan and Edward Heath 'inhabit a never-never land where it would be possible – given "moderation" on all sides – to enjoy the sweetness of inflating the currency without suffering the punishment which follows'.[10] The great battle in the Conservative Party which erupted when Margaret Thatcher replaced Edward Heath as leader in 1976 and is only now starting to subside, really began in 1959 when Macmillan accepted Thorneycroft's resignation. The 'one nation' Conservatives had won the first round, but not the last. Macmillan appointed a new Chancellor, Derek Heathcoat Amory, and departed for a five-

After his resignation in 1958, John Enoch Powell (1912–98) returned to government as Minister of Health in 1960, where, among other initiatives, he was responsible for recruiting large numbers of Commonwealth immigrants into the understaffed NHS. In 1965 he stood for the Conservative leadership against Heath, but came a distant third. While Shadow Defence Secretary, he made his infamous 'Rivers of Blood' speech against immigration in 1968, and Heath sacked him. In 1974 Powell left the Conservative Party over EEC membership, and joined the Ulster Unionists.

week tour of the Commonwealth, remarking airily on *these little local difficulties*.

That was the measure of his new-found confidence. He was now a Prime Minster in full control of his Cabinet, whom the public had grown to like and trust – his patrician style appealed to a nation which still like to be patronised by the gentry – and who had now surrounded himself with a small and trusted group of advisers, including his old friend John Wyndham, who had first worked for him at the Ministry of Supply. His method of working was measured and calm, and took 10 Downing Street back to the businesslike days of Clement Attlee, before the unpredictable Churchill and the frenetic Eden. His family life was as good as it was ever likely to be: the sexual passion between his wife and Robert Boothby was more or less spent and she was his emotional mainstay, almost his link with real life, with her earthy, unintellectual common sense. He enjoyed taking advantage of the fact that during the week the Prime Minister lives above the shop to see more of his young grandchildren than he had seen of his own children when they were young.

*... these little local difficulties.*

MACMILLAN

There were differences with the Americans over China and the Middle East, but this time the personal relationship between Macmillan and Eisenhower, as well as Macmillan's realistic estimate of the balance of power between them, kept them from becoming crises. He helped engineer a settlement of the Cyprus crisis, with Cyprus becoming an independent republic under Greek Cypriot president, Makarios, and a Turkish Cypriot vice president. He obtained from the Americans something that had eluded Attlee, Churchill and Eden – a common nuclear programme between Britain and the USA. And in February 1959, with the approval both of

President Eisenhower and the main European leaders, he went to the Soviet Union for meetings with its new leader, Nikita Khrushchev, designed to pave the way for a meeting of western foreign ministers and ultimately a summit. The splendid fur hat he had worn in wartime Finland was reclaimed from the Macmillan grandchildren for the trip, and became part of the Macmillan image.

*Most people in this country have never had it so good.*

MACMILLAN

Better economic news in January 1959 paved the way for an election budget, with reductions in income tax and purchase tax. His new Conservative Party chairman, Lord Hailsham, provided the showmanship he knew was needed – Hailsham famously rang a large bell during his speech at the party conference – and spent £500,000 on advertising. A short, sharp slogan was invented – 'Life's better with the Conservatives, don't let Labour ruin it' – which echoed a famous Prime Ministerial remark that *most people in this country have never had it so good*. Eisenhower, now once again willing to help the Conservatives to victory as he had done in 1955, came to Britain for five days and appeared on television with the Prime Minister, giving the appearance of two elderly, trusted statesmen making the world a safer place. The cartoonist Vicky christened the Prime Minister 'Supermac', and on 8 October he won a stunning election victory which would have been thought inconceivable just two years earlier, with 365 seats against Labour's 258.

# Chapter 9: Plucking Defeat from the Jaws of Victory (1959–63)

Britain's crumbling African empire played little part in the 1959 election, but constituted the most urgent problem for the new government. Black Africans were serving notice of the end of Empire, with disturbances in Kenya, Nyasaland, Southern Rhodesia and Northern Rhodesia, which the white government greeted in the way they believed natives should be handled, with instant repression.

That same year, de Gaulle – now installed as French president with a new constitution giving him much greater powers – shocked his nation, and especially his supporters, by offering Algeria self-determination. If he had not known it before, Macmillan certainly knew now that the days of Britain's dwindling African empire were numbered. But this was not a thought to be shared with a party whose soul was still in the patrician care of the likes of Lord Salisbury.

Even less was it a thought to be shared with Sir Roy Welensky, Prime Minister of the Central African Federation, which comprised Nyasaland and Northern and Southern Rhodesia. A former heavyweight boxing champion of Rhodesia and train driver, with a Polish-Jewish father and an Afrikaner mother, Welensky's answer to a British television interviewer who asked if he understood the African mind was: 'Considering that when I was a lad I swam bare-arsed in the Makabusi with the piccanins, I think I can say I know something about Africans.'[1] He amused Lord Home, the Commonwealth Secretary, with stories about how he hired African sparring partners for a penny each, tiring after 50 of them.

The Federation, created just six years earlier, was deeply unpopular with Africans, and Macmillan set up a commission under Sir Walter Monckton to enquire into its future. Monckton's report, to Welensky's fury, called for a broader franchise, an African majority in the legislature of Northern Rhodesia, and for Britain to allow the secession of any territory which wished it. Meanwhile a judge, Sir Patrick Devlin, was appointed to investigate the disturbances, and sensationally reported that 'Nyasaland is – no doubt temporarily – a police state'.

As Colonial Secretary Macmillan appointed one of the brightest of the new high flyers, 45-year-old Iain Macleod. Sir Roy Welensky did not understand the significance of this appointment until it was much, much too late, but Macmillan knew what he was doing. 'It has been said,' Macleod wrote later, 'that after I became Colonial Secretary, there was a deliberate speeding up of the movement towards independence. I agree. There was. And in my view any other policy would have led to terrible bloodshed in Africa.'[2] Nor did Welensky understand the significance of Macmillan's decision to tour Africa early in 1960. The boxer had met his match. Years later he described Macmillan ruefully: 'As soothing as cream and as sharp as a razor.'[3] Macmillan's old friend, fellow Etonian and Grenadier, now his enemy, Lord Salisbury, understood it better. Macleod, he told the House of Lords, had successfully set out to outwit the

*'As soothing as cream and as sharp as a razor.'*

WELENSKY ON MACMILLAN

'white people' of Africa. 'He has been too clever by half,' he added, with withering patrician contempt.[4]

Macmillan began his tour in newly independent Ghana and Nigeria, where he gave everyone the impression he was ready to see majority rule in all of Britain's African empire, then made his way to Salisbury, the capital of the Federation, where he managed to give exactly the opposite impression; and thence to South Africa, where he was to address both Houses of Parliament. No one knew what a bombshell this speech was to be. Journalist Anthony Sampson was there: 'It began with elaborate compliments to South Africa's progress and courage in war, and quietly led on to an exposition of African nationalism: *The most striking of all the impressions I have formed since I left London a month ago is of the strength of this African national consciousness. In different places it may take different forms, but it is happening everywhere. The wind of change is blowing through this continent ... As a fellow member of the Commonwealth, it is our earnest desire to give South Africa our support and encouragement, but I hope you won't mind my saying frankly that there are some aspects of your policies which make it impossible for us to do this without being false to our own deep convictions about the political destinies of free men* . . He then concluded – as if he had been saying nothing very much – with an attack on boycotts and some conventional sentiments about the Commonwealth. It was a speech of masterly construction and phrasing, beautifully spoken, combining a sweep of history with unambiguous political points. It was probably the finest of Macmillan's career.'[5]

*The wind of change is blowing through this continent ...*

MACMILLAN

Back in London in February, Macmillan took on an entirely unnecessary battle. He was invited to stand for Chancellor of Oxford University. Oxford politics being a Byzantine business, the purpose of Macmillan's backers was to see off the establishment candidate, Sir Oliver Franks. It was a considerable risk for little reward, but Macmillan relished the fight and really wanted the job, and he stood for it and won. It was a symbol of his great and growing confidence, for he risked a humiliating rebuff. With a huge parliamentary majority, facing a Labour opposition which was depressed, demoralised and divided, with Conservative MPs believing they owed their startling election victory (and in many cases their seats) to him, Macmillan, like the voters, had never had it so good. Prime Ministers need to be wary of feeling good. As Macmillan famously recognised later, what really dictates to government is *events, dear boy, events*. Selwyn Lloyd's 1961 budget was followed by a sterling crisis. The Chancellor quickly brought in a 'pay pause' to stop wages from fuelling inflation, and squeezed government spending. The feelgood factor which had brought the Conservatives their magnificent election victory melted like snow in the springtime.

Meanwhile Macmillan was moving towards his biggest gamble: his application for British membership of the European Economic Community (EEC). He put out careful private feelers in Europe, and raised it when he visited the new American president, John F Kennedy, in Washington. Kennedy was unexpectedly positive about the idea, seeing the chance that Britain might influence the rather less pro-American governments of France and Germany. Armed with permission from Kennedy, Macmillan authorised Edward Heath to advocate an application for membership, and in Autumn that year, 1961, Heath led the British negotiating team in an application.

Negotiations were still under way in March 1962 when three by-elections showed just how much the economic crisis had shaken confidence in the government. The Conservative vote fell by between 10,000 and 15,000 and the safe seat of Orpington fell to the Liberals. The Conservatives were suffering from something more than the realisation that Macmillan, though undoubtedly clever, was not 'Supermac'. Iain Macleod believed that after Suez, the Conservatives lost the intellectual vote. Something certainly changed fundamentally in the British national psyche. Perhaps the 1960s really began with *Look Back in Anger* in the summer of 1956, only no one noticed until 1962 when the Beatles released *Love Me Do*. Perhaps they really began in November 1956 with Suez, but it took the 1964 election of Harold Wilson – the first Prime Minister not to have been in Churchill's wartime government – before anyone noticed.

**John F Kennedy** (1917–63), 35th President of the United States, was both the youngest man and the only Catholic to be elected President when he came to office in 1961, defeating the Republican Richard Nixon in a close race marred by allegations of vote-rigging. His presidency saw the botched invasion of Cuba (the Bay of Pigs), the Cuban Missile Crisis and increased American military involvement in Vietnam. His assassination in Dallas on 22 November 1963 was one of the defining moments of United States' history and gave rise to conspiracy theories that have continued to this day.

Certainly the walls of respect were being breached. By the time Macmillan lost Orpington, Peter Cook had been standing for several months on the stage of the Fortune Theatre in London's West End, performing his famous imitation of the Prime Minister. Today it would seem relatively mild, but at the time it was groundbreaking in its disrespect. It had a perceptive view of Britain's post-Suez impotence and reliance on American support, as well as of the relationship between Macmillan and President Kennedy: 'I then went on to America, and there I had talks

## Europe

'Since 1944 Charles de Gaulle had nursed the idea that Europe could become a major forced, ultimately "the most powerful, prosperous and influential political, economic, cultural and military grouping in the world". He called for a "European Europe", a western-European bloc free of foreign (that is, American) domination.

De Gaulle was convinced that Europe offered great possibilities to France. As he told one minister in 1962: "Europe is the chance for France to become what she has ceased to be since Waterloo: the first in the world." The English console themselves for their decline by saying that they are in American hegemony. Germany has had her backbone broken." It followed from this that France was, for the moment at least, "the third international reality ... the only one at the moment, apart from the Americans and Russians, to have an ambition for the nation."

De Gaulle provided cogent reasons for blocking British entry which were shared by many who deplored the brutal style of the French veto: Britain's links with the Commonwealth, her tradition of free trade, and her small agricultural sector would, he argued, fit badly into a protectionist continental bloc with important agricultural interests. His main fear was that Britain would be an American Trojan horse in his "European Europe". Macmillan was startled to be reminded by de Gaulle of Churchill's remark about always choosing the open sea before Europe. De Gaulle's view of Britain was reinforced when the Americans cancelled production of the Skybolt missiles and Macmillan accepted Kennedy's offer to replace them with American-produced Polaris missiles integrated into a multilateral NATO force. Although Macmillan had obtained the same offer for France, de Gaulle saw this as definitive proof of British dependence on America. De Gaulle's unspoken reason for opposing British entry was the fear that it would threaten his vision of a Europe under Franco-German leadership, with Germany as the junior partner.' [Julian Jackson, *De Gaulle* (Haus Publishing, London: 2003) p 98ff.]

with the young, vigorous president [here Cook would sound dreadfully old and weary] and danced with his very lovely lady wife. We talked of many things, including Great Britain's position in the world as some kind of honest broker. I agreed with him, when he said that no nation could be more honest; and he agreed with me, when I chaffed him and said that no nation could be broker. This kind of genial, statesmanlike banter often went on late into the night.' As for the American missiles Kennedy promised Macmillan, 'A very handsome weapon, we shall be very proud to have them – the photographs, I mean, we shan't get the missiles until around 1970 – in the meantime we shall have to keep our fingers crossed, sit very quietly and try not to alienate anyone.'

Macmillan went to the Fortune Theatre and declared himself delighted, but he was the first Prime Minister for years to be mocked in this way, and the magic had gone out of his premiership. He and his government were looking older, tireder, and a little out of touch. Iain Macleod, the most perceptive observer of the popular mood available to Macmillan, wrote to him after the loss of Orpington: 'One thing that emerges with absolute clarity is that the popular reasons such as pensions, Schedule A, nuclear disarmament and colonial policy had nothing

**Peter Cook** (1937–95) was a genuine comic genius. After appearing in *Beyond the Fringe*, in 1961 he opened the Establishment Club in London as a venue for satirical comedy, and in 1964 became the main backer of *Private Eye*. He later starred in the TV series *Not Only ... But Also*, with Dudley Moore and their partnership as 'Pete n' Dud' became a comedy legend. However, in the 1970s and 1980s his career stalled due in part to alcoholism, just as Moore's Hollywood career took off. There were signs of a revival in the early 1990s, but he died in 1995 of severe liver damage.

whatever to do with the result. Incomparably the leading factor was the dislike of the Government.' A great deal would hang 'both on the budget and on the words that the Chancellor uses'.[6]

The Prime Minister liked his Chancellor Selwyn Lloyd, but wanted an election-winning budget in 1963, not a task for which Lloyd's careful, conservative character and personality suited him. Lloyd's 1962 budget was cautious and cautiously presented, and he seemed unwilling to do anything radically different the next year, since he thought expansion would produce damaging inflation. After the budget, pressure grew for the Prime Minister to sack his Chancellor, along with a few other ministers to give his government a younger image.

But when he finally did the deed, in July 1962, Macmillan did it in the clumsiest and most damaging way. It was not entirely his fault. On 11 July Rab Butler, whom Macmillan had taken into his confidence, indiscreetly let the *Daily Mail* know that Lloyd was to go. Macmillan thought this forced him to act at once, and the very next day he abruptly fired Lloyd and six other Cabinet ministers. Lloyd was not offered any other Cabinet post. He had, most people felt, been treated very badly, and Macmillan had panicked. 'Greater love hath no man than this', said a young Liberal MP (and future Liberal leader) Jeremy Thorpe, 'than he lay down his friends for his life.' Right-wing Conservatives like Health Minister Enoch Powell saw it as yet another proof that the Prime Minister was, as they suspected all along, a closet Bolshevik, and Powell sneered later about Macmillan policies designed as 'a quid pro quo to the workers for co-operation in an inflation-free planned economy. I still relish recalling how the heads which were to roll not long after

*'Greater love hath no man than this, than he lay down his friends for his life.'*
JEREMY THORPE

nodded like cuckoo clocks in sycophantic approval'.[7] Many Conservatives, especially on the right of the party, thought, as Selwyn Lloyd's biographer wrote later, that it was 'shameful and personally wounding ... the unworthiest moment of Macmillan's entire premiership'.[8]

In Reginald Maudling, Macmillan found the Chancellor he wanted: able, unorthodox, young, a man who would deliver expansion, and who understood that Macmillan's desire for expansion was as much dictated by the hardship he had seen in Stockton as by electoral advantage. He was stout, comfortable and a little cynical: Macmillan once said that Maudling wouldn't go to the stake for anything unless it was well covered in Bearnaise sauce. Maudling might be able to deliver a budget that might help win the next election, but could not deliver a new role for Macmillan's increasingly dissatisfied nation. On 5 December 1962, US Secretary of State Dean Rusk delivered a speech so brutally honest that he has never been forgiven for it: 'Great Britain has lost an empire and has not yet found a role. The attempt to play a separate power role – that is, a role apart from Europe, a role based on a "special relationship" with the United States, a role based on being the head of a "Commonwealth" which has no political structure, unity or strength and enjoys a fragile and precarious economic relationship by means of the sterling area and preferences in the British market – this role is absolutely played out.'[9] More than three decades after Dean Rusk brutally but accurately consigned it to history, an aide to President Bill Clinton reminded him, as he was about to meet the British press, to mention the special relationship. 'Oh, yes' said Clinton. 'How could I forget? The special relationship.' And he laughed.[10] But Britain is still not ready to throw off its comfort blanket.

Rusk's speech, cruelly, came less than two months after

## The Special Relationship

*Memorandum of telephone conversation between President Kennedy and Prime Minister Macmillan, 22 October, 1962*

The clandestine way that the Soviets have made their build-up in Cuba would have unhinged us in all of Latin America. To allow it to continue would have thrown into question all our statements about Berlin.

*PM spoke.*

We have the potential to occupy Cuba but we didn't start that way. There would be a gap of some days before invasion could be mounted. Preparations for invasion would have public notice. This way provides action without immediate escalation to war. Action is limited now. Greater force would give him the same excuse in Berlin. It may be necessary to expand blockade to include fuel, lubricants and so forth.

*PM spoke* (about possible Russian action).

He may require us to seize their ships by force. There is no telling what he will do – probably it will be something in Berlin.

*PM spoke* (about talking to K on phone).

No, but I sent a letter to him one hour ago. Khrushchev is playing a double game. He said he wasn't going to do anything until after the election. He said weapons in Cuba were not offensive. It is obvious that he was attempting to face us in November with a bad situation.

*PM spoke.*

Some action was necessary. It would result in WWIII; we could lose Berlin.

*PM spoke.*

Invasion may yet be required. It requires seven days for mobilization of the necessary forces. In any event we won't invade until I speak again with you.

*PM spoke.*

It faces Khrushchev with action taken which has unpleasant options for him also.'

[Tim Coates (ed), *The Cuban Missile Crisis, 1962* (The Stationary Office, London: 2001) pp 231ff.]

the Cuban missile crisis. During the great standoff between Kennedy and Khrushchev over Soviet weapons based in Cuba, Kennedy kept in close private touch with Macmillan, whom he respected personally, but Macmillan had to appear to be out of the loop. 'Why wasn't Macmillan told about Cuba?' asked the new satirical magazine *Private Eye*, launched on the back of the success of *Beyond the Fringe*; and the magazine gave its answer in tiny type at the foot of the page: 'He was, but he forgot.' Yet in 1962, Harold Macmillan and Edward Heath thought they had the answer to Rusk. British membership of the EEC, short-sightedly ignored by all Macmillan's predecessors, was to bring Britain economic stability, a new role in the world, and renewed self-esteem.

It was not to be. Five weeks after Rusk's speech, on 14 January 1963, Macmillan's old friend General de Gaulle, whom Macmillan had so loyally and skilfully protected from the wrath of Churchill and Roosevelt during the war, destroyed what was to have been Macmillan's greatest triumph. He vetoed British membership. He could not, he said, believe that Britain was ready to put its European friends before its Commonwealth, its American friends, and its European Free Trade Area partners. He had a point.

De Gaulle, Rusk and Cuba had shown Britain's irrelevance, the winter was one of the longest and coldest anyone could remember, and Labour's lead in the Gallup poll was the highest for 17 years. Macmillan's crusty old Tory enemies were circling, and the young appeared to have nothing but scorn for him. He was visibly ageing. Things were looking black for his premiership even before the Profumo affair burst over his head.

John Profumo was one of the Conservative Party's brightest young stars, promoted to Defence Minister very early as one of the beneficiaries of the 'night of the long knives'. Rumours that Profumo was having an affair with Christine Keeler, a 'call girl' who had also been sleeping with a Soviet embassy official, had been circulating for months. When the Labour opposition started to raise them in the House of Commons, Profumo was forced to account for himself, first to the cabinet and then to the House, where he said in March 1963: 'There was no impropriety whatsoever in my acquaintanceship with Miss Keeler.' In June, he was forced to admit that he had lied to the House. He had to go.

The press was able to pretend that what really mattered was not the sex, but the supposed security implications of the Defence Minister sharing a mistress with a Soviet official. In the same way, when a civil servant, William Vassall, was sentenced to 18 years imprisonment for spying in 1962, newspapers were able to say that their interest lay, not in Vassall's homosexuality, but in the fact that this made him vulnerable to blackmail by Soviet spies. In both cases, the result was the same: endless stories about sex. The government started to look as though it was up to its neck in sex, spies and sleaze, and the Prime Minister seemed too elderly and out of touch to know what was going on.

On one side, he could hear the raucous sound of cruel laughter from the young. On the other – as one of the satirists, Bernard Levin, a regular on the BBC's new late night Saturday show *That Was The Week That Was*, put it – there were 'armies of Pharisees marching in their holy wrath; and of these the commander in chief, beyond a doubt, was Lord Hailsham'. The man Macmillan had made Party Chairman to put some oomph into its campaigning now put a lot of oomph into self-righteous indignation. Levin wrote: 'In one passage alone he called Mr Profumo a liar seven times in 90 words.' Levin added that in his final sentence – 'A great party is not to be brought down because of a scandal by a woman of easy virtue and a proved liar' – Hailsham said the word 'liar' 'with such manic violence that those watching might have thought that he was about to go completely berserk'. Hailsham probably deserved one of the cruellest rebukes ever offered to a politician, at the hands of Reginald Paget MP, who said men like Hailsham (a portly man) 'compound for sins they are inclined to by damning those they have no mind to,' adding: 'When self-indulgence has reduced a man to the shape of Lord Hailsham, sexual continence involves no more than a sense of the ridiculous.'[11]

The young thought the Prime Minister was ludicrous and out-of-touch. The old, represented by the leader columns of *The Times*, thought this display of sexual self-indulgence was all the fault of the 'never had it so good' society the Prime Minister had encouraged. Either way it was all Macmillan's fault, and the Labour leader Harold Wilson seemed like the sort of modern, efficient man who could dig the country out of Macmillan's genteel quagmire.

Whether the old master could have turned it round one last time, we will never know. He enjoyed a triumph with the negotiation of a nuclear test ban treaty, but this did not stop plotting in the party to replace him. Macmillan was undecided, but on 8 October, just before the Conservative Party conference, he telephoned Buckingham Palace to say that he had decided to stay on and fight another election. What he did not tell the Palace was that he had woken during the night in severe pain, unable to pass water. But when the Cabinet met that morning, ministers could see that he looked ill and in pain, and he left the room rather often.

After the Cabinet a surgeon saw the Prime Minister and told him that he needed surgery for an inflamed prostate. And straight away, Macmillan knew he was going to resign. He did not have to; he was told that the inflammation was not cancerous, and the operation had every prospect of success. But he knew how serious his political problems were, he knew he was not as strong or healthy as he had been, and he knew that many of his Cabinet wanted him to go. He regretted the decision later, and some commentators have suggested that he thought he had cancer and might die, but the truth is that, at that moment, it almost seemed like a blessing in disguise, making it easier to take a decision that, in his heart, he wanted to take.

That day, Macmillan and his ministers were due to travel to Blackpool for the Conservative Party conference. The first person to know Macmillan's decision was Lord Home, the Foreign Secretary and Macmillan's closest friend in the Cabinet, who visited Macmillan in hospital. Home thought the speculation had reached fever pitch, and there should be an announcement. Butler, who suspected the truth, despatched a message from Blackpool saying that he hoped there would be no reference to the leadership during the conference. In the advice from both these men there was an element of shrewd calculation. A decision during the conference would favour Home, who was not generally thought to be a candidate but was popular with rank and file Conservatives; and even more, Lord Hailsham, the noisy, plummy, bombastic voice always associated with the Tory Party. A vote after the conference would favour Butler, who was popular among MPs. The field was very wide, and the party could decide to go for the younger men. The most obvious of them was Maudling, though Edward Heath and Iain Macleod were possibles at the start. Home's view prevailed, and he carried to Blackpool a letter from the Prime Minister to read to the assembled delegates. The fact that Macmillan entrusted Home with the task of telling the conference may have been – probably was – an indication of the direction in which his mind was already moving.

There were no processes for electing a new leader. The procedure used in 1957, when a couple of grandees invited key people into their room and asked whether it was 'Wab or Hawold,' could not cope with so large a field. In any case, the fact that the party conference was starting made it impossible to do the thing discreetly.

Hailsham was first in the queue for the job, announcing that very evening that he had decided to renounce his peerage so that he could take on the job, should anyone offer it to him. (He and Home could be candidates only because of the recent legislation which had allowed Tony Benn to renounce his peerage.) This was followed by lapel buttons with the letter 'Q' and a photo call with his infant child. It all looked a little undignified to Macmillan. Senior figures in the Party made pilgrimages to Home's hotel room to ask him to stand. The key supporter seems to have been Selwyn Lloyd, who went about the conference quietly urging on everyone he spoke to the virtues of the Foreign Secretary. Home himself delivered a speech in the foreign affairs debate that pressed every Conservative button there was, and sat down to a rapturous reception. By contrast, Maudling's economic speech provoked little enthusiasm.

Butler was due to stand in for Macmillan and give the leader's speech at the end of the conference, and that day he and his wife lunched with the Homes. Home said he was seeing his doctor the next week 'because I have been approached about the possibility of my becoming the Leader of the Conservative Party'.[12] It came as a nasty shock to Butler when he was already anxious and nervous, and his speech was not a success.

The week after the conference, Macmillan took a hand. He outlined procedures for consultation in a memorandum he sent to Butler to be reported to the Cabinet. Then began the famous procession of senior figures to his hospital bedside, starting with Home who confirmed that he was willing to stand, and provided the information that the Americans were not impressed by Hailsham. Macmillan, having rescued the government after Suez, was not about to put into Downing Street a man who did not have friends in Washington; and he had been shocked by Hailsham's behaviour at the conference.

> *Lord Home is clearly a man who represents the old, governing class at its best and those who take a reasonably impartial view of English history know how good that can be…*
>
> MACMILLAN

He saw everyone who mattered, and at last was ready to place his recommendation in the hands of the Queen. It was Lord Home. Macmillan always claimed that all he did was to report the views he was given, and the political arithmetic these led to, but there is no doubt that to some extent he influenced the views which were then relayed to him, not least by arranging that Lord Home should read his statement to the conference. The decision accorded with Macmillan's own wishes. An early draft of the memorandum he wrote for the Queen contained truly revealing passages which were expunged from the later, official, draft the Queen actually received, and it is pure Macmillan – at one and the same time thoughtful, snobbish and patrician: *Lord Home is clearly a man who represents the old, governing class at its best and those who take a reasonably impartial view of English history know how good that can be ... Had he been of another generation, he would have been of the Grenadiers and the 1914 heroes ... It is interesting that he has proved himself so much liked by men like President Kennedy and Mr Rusk and Mr Gromyko. This is exactly the quality that the class to which he belongs have at their best because they think about the question under discussion and not about themselves. It is thinking about themselves that is really the curse of the younger generation – they appear to have no other subject which interests them at all and all their books, poems, dramas and all the rest of it are almost entirely confined to this curious, introspective attitude towards life ...*[13] Perhaps Peter Cook and Bernard Levin were right, after all.

# Part Three

## THE LEGACY

# Chapter 10: 'Selling the family silver' (1963–86)

Lord Home, quickly transmogrified into Sir Alec Douglas-Home MP, narrowly lost the 1964 general election to Harold Wilson's Labour Party. Macmillan spoke only three times in the House of Commons before the election. One of these was a heartbroken tribute the day after President Kennedy was assassinated. He did not stand for Parliament again, but refused to go to the House of Lords. After a lifetime of being almost a part of the real aristocracy he so admired, it would have felt like a step backwards to take a life peerage as though he was some wealthy parvenu.

Macmillan lived another 23 years, long enough to see the Conservative Party he had done as much as Churchill to create first triumphant under Macmillan's protégé Edward Heath, then crushed by a resurgence of the tradition of Lord Salisbury and Enoch Powell led by Margaret Thatcher. He determined to stay out of politics, saying characteristically: *It is tempting, perhaps, but unrewarding to hang about the greenroom after final retirement from the stage.* He did at last succumb to the temptation, but not during the first 16 years of his retirement, when Number 10 was occupied by first Harold Wilson for Labour, then Edward Heath for the Conservatives, then Wilson and James Callaghan for Labour. In those years the post-war consensus, created by Attlee and Churchill and cemented by Macmillan, was not threatened. Had he ever had the smallest doubt about Edward Heath, it would have been dissipated when Heath was attacked by Lord Salisbury, to cheers from backwoodsmen at the 1965 Conservative Party conference, for colluding with the Wilson government over imposing sanctions on 'our friends and kinfolk', the Rhodesian whites.

*It is tempting, perhaps, but unrewarding to hang about the greenroom after final retirement from the stage.*

MACMILLAM

Three years after his retirement, Macmillan's wife died from a sudden and massive heart attack at the age of 66, the same age as the century. The countrywoman had had only three years of retirement to immerse herself in her beautiful garden at Birch Grove, at last getting away from London, which she hated. Despite the problems in their marriage, she really had been his rock, his best friend, the person who sustained his spirits, and he missed her dreadfully: her joie de vivre, her naturalness, her spirit, and perhaps her aristocratic confidence, which, despite all he had achieved, was still a thing he envied. The Boothby affair had been a lasting scar, but they overcame it to have a splendid Indian summer in their marriage from about 1960 on. After Dorothy's death there was no late flowering of love for Macmillan, though he enjoyed the company of women *who make me feel safe*. Still the shy pubic school bachelor with only a semi-detached interest in sex, he found forceful women rather frightening, and made an enemy of Dame Rebecca West by turning his back on her at a literary luncheon and talking throughout to the woman on the other side of him.

Macmillan regretted his decision to retire, and wanted to work. He took over as chairman of the family publishing house until his son Maurice replaced him in 1967, and then took over again from 1970 to 1974 while Maurice was a minister in Edward Heath's government. His Chancellorship of Oxford University became much more than the sinecure it had been while he was Prime Minister: he transformed the role, fundraising in the USA and dining in all the colleges. These and the writing of his six volumes of memoirs (it started out as three) of two million words, and his several London clubs, kept him fully occupied.

He proved remarkably quick at adapting to the changes in publishing since he last worked there, and as before, he took risks and brought the company back to profitability. Muriel Spark was one of his authors and remembered: 'He was enormously intelligent and full of humour, even when he wryly referred to himself as *a fallen minister*. I remember I once had to meet him somewhere in London and was holding the *Evening Standard*, which I had bought on the way. Harold pointed to the picture on the front page. It was of Nikita Khrushchev, now also out of office, casting his vote in one of their so-called elections. *Just look at him*, said Harold. *How well they've turned him out. A smart coat, a good hat ... My government never gave me a good hat*. Harold really did have a very charming smile. Just to see him smile I liked to make him laugh.'

His wit flowered in retirement, when he no longer had to guard his tongue, and some of the most famous aphorisms come from this period in his life. One day, three former premiers – Macmillan, Home and Wilson, according to the version I heard – arrived together for a Privy Council meeting. Wilson said: 'I wonder what the collective noun is for a group of former Prime Ministers?' And Macmillan replied: *A lack of principals, I should imagine*.

As he got older, he lived mostly in a small, spartan room in the attic of Birch Grove. Increasingly, like all of us, the older he got the more funerals he had to attend, and he described them (quoting the actor Ralph Richardson) as the *cocktail parties of the geriatric set*. Sadly, these funerals included those of his daughter Sarah and his son Maurice. Sarah's short life was not a happy one. Biologically Robert Boothby's daughter, she was devoted to the only father she knew, Macmillan, and horrified when she discovered the truth about her parentage when she was in her late teens. An abortion – forced on her, it is said, by her mother because an illegitimate child would ruin Macmillan's career – left her unable to have children, and she adopted two children but was never really able to look after them, and after Dorothy's death Macmillan spent a lot of time with them. She had the Devonshire disease of alcoholism, and, like her brother Maurice, made several trips to Switzerland to be dried out, but in her case without success. Macmillan frequently traveled out to see her, and she was full of remorse for the trouble she caused him. She died in 1970. Maurice fell ill and died in March 1984. By then, Macmillan had given way to the temptation to walk the stage again.

He was no longer chairman of Macmillans, he had written his memoirs and he was watching the beginning of the victory of the monetarists in the Conservative Party, with Margaret Thatcher driving Edward Heath from the leadership. Increasingly, right-wing Conservatives were looking back to the Macmillan era as the time when everything went to pot. So after Mrs Thatcher became Prime Minister in 1979, his pronouncements became more frequent, and more acerbic. He was horrified by her anti-Europeanism. He was appalled by wholesale privatisation. Monetarism he thought a cruel, unimaginative economic policy. Most of all, he hated the Thatcher attitude to trade unions. For Macmillan, there had always been two sides to industry, and, snobbish as he may have been about union leaders, he had always accepted them as the authentic voice of the working class, to which enlightened capitalists should listen. It was that subject which provoked his first speech in the House of Lords.

In 1984, during the Miners' Strike, he at last accepted a peerage – the first hereditary peerage for many years – and became the Earl of Stockton. This was a statement in itself, for Stockton was the working-class constituency where he had learned to care about poverty, and which rejected him for Labour in 1945. But it was also a statement that he intended to take a more active role in criticising government policy. Horrified by the way he could see the miners being ground down, in his first speech to the Lords he said that the strike was being fought by *the best men in the world. They beat the Kaiser's army and they beat Hitler's army. They never gave in.*

All his old Tory enemies – from Lord Salisbury to Enoch Powell to Margaret Thatcher – saw that the old charmer was still a bounder. Their spokesman for posterity, historian Andrew Roberts, fulminates on their behalf: 'When Macmillan was recovering from being shot in the hand in September 1916, "the best men in the world" were withdrawing their labour ... over wage rates greatly in excess of what Captain Macmillan's men were receiving ...'.[1] The next year, 1985, Macmillan re-entered the fray, calling Thatcher's privatisations *selling the family silver*.

*Selling the family silver.*
MACMILLAN ON PRIVATISATION

But by then he was growing very frail, and had pleurisy, shingles and gout. He knew he was not long for the world, and was unafraid, though rather pleased he had managed to go on believing in God. *If you don't believe in God, all you have to believe in is decency. Decency is very good. Better decent than indecent. But I don't think it's enough*, he once said. He died at Birch Grove on 29 December 1986, and his grandson Alexander Macmillan succeeded to the Earldom of Stockton.

# Chapter 11: The Last Edwardian, the First Moderniser

Harold Macmillan was the bridge along which we walked from Edwardian England to Thatcher's Britain; from wartime austerity to the Swinging Sixties. He was the last gentleman premier, the last to have seen the inside of a Flanders trench, the last to have stood side by side with Winston during the war and shared his fears and dangers, the last to have known Lloyd George and grown up with the poetry of Rudyard Kipling. But he was the first to understand the radically changed world, to realise the power of television and learn its techniques, to know what Harold Wilson meant by the 'white heat of technology'.

He could perform this ambiguous role because he was a wonderfully ambiguous man – it is no wonder that the first biography to be published, by Anthony Sampson in 1967, is called *Macmillan – a study in ambiguity*. He was an old-fashioned class-conscious patrician Tory, who sneered about the middle classes and about trade union leaders in their oh-so-respectable suits and hats. Yet he had a romanticised ideal of the British working man – *the salt of the earth* – and could not bear to see him forced into poverty and deprived of dignity. An Edwardian Tory, with all the Edwardian assumptions about the moral value of material success, and the Edwardian dislike of taxing the rich to feed the poor, in the 1930s he was an early advocate of what became known as the Welfare State. An Edwardian patriot who thought Britain ruled the waves, he was the first Prime Minister to accept the post-war reality that Britain didn't even rule her own backyard: the first to go to Washington as a visible supplicant, the first to ask Europe if we could please come and shelter under their umbrella.

It is what he represented, rather than what he achieved, that make Macmillan one of the great Prime Ministers of the 20th century. He was not an Attlee or a Thatcher, changing by sheer determination and clarity of purpose the way the nation lived. He did not make change so much as manage it, but he did that well and effectively. What determined your priorities, was, as he put it, *events, dear boy, events* – but whether events are positive or negative often depends on who is minding the shop when they happen.

National self-esteem was probably never lower than when Macmillan became Prime Minister in 1957. He did all the humiliating things he had to do, while sustaining and nurturing his country's pride. He went to Washington with head held high, and took whatever crumbs he was given – an English gentleman, albeit in reduced circumstances – and his countrymen cheered, and felt a patriotic glow in their hearts, and called him 'Supermac'.

One of those childhood memories that will always be with me – along with Tony Hancock saying 'A man of my cal-i-bre' and Richard Greene outwitting the Sheriff of Nottingham – is Macmillan standing at the United Nations rostrum while the vulgar fat Russian communist Nikita Khrushchev banged his shoe on the table and shrieked in some dreadful foreign language, being, naturally, insufficiently educated to shout in English.

*Could we have a translation of that please?*

MACMILLAN

Macmillan, waited until he had finished and then, with that deadly English upper-class courtesy which speaks volumes of contempt to those in the know, he said: *Could we have a translation of that please?* For one moment, the least patriotic among us wanted to wave our Union Jacks, though not with any vulgar display, of course.

He is rightly criticised for Suez, where he fully deserved Harold Wilson's pointed criticism that he was 'first in, first out'. But he was also, probably, the only person who could get the country – and the Conservative Party – out of the hole he had helped dig. A man with his views could only have flourished in the Conservative Party of the post-Second World War period, when Winston Churchill had committed himself to the general principles of the wartime Beveridge Report. The Conservative Party did not contest the post-war consensus until 1979, and Macmillan and Edward Heath (who beat Iain Macleod and Reginald Maudling for the leadership in 1965) were both in favour of it.

Ideologically, Macmillan and Heath were soulmates. Heath would have made as little progress in the Conservative Party of the 1930s as Macmillan, and Macmillan as little in the 1980s as Heath. They were far too left-wing. Like Macmillan, Heath was passionately opposed to Chamberlain and appeasement at the end of the 1930s. Like Macmillan, he supported A D Lindsay (who was his tutor – like Macmillan, Heath was a Balliol man) as the anti-appeasement candidate in the 1938 Oxford by-election. Like Macmillan, he believed the trade unions had a key role in industry. A committed European from the start, Heath made his maiden speech in the House of Commons in 1948 in favour of the Schuman Plan, the predecessor of the Common Market. He carried on Macmillan's policy of disengagement from Rhodesia, earning the contempt of Macmillan's former friend and present enemy, Lord Salisbury. And, just as Macmillan would have done, he declined to profit from the widespread dislike of black immigrants which was encouraged by Enoch Powell's 'rivers of blood' speech in 1968, instead firing Powell from his Shadow Cabinet. As soon as he became Prime Minister in 1970, he made Britain's third application to join the European Community, and was at last successful. He used public money to support big companies in trouble, in order to stave off unemployment.

Heath admired Macmillan greatly. He wrote: 'Harold Macmillan had by far the most constructive mind I have encountered in a lifetime of politics. He took a fully informed view of both domestic and world affairs, and would put the tiniest local problem into a national context, and any national problem into its rightful position in his world strategy. Macmillan's historical knowledge enabled him to view everything in a realistic perspective, and to illuminate contemporary questions with both parallels and differences in comparison with the past. His mind was cultivated in many disciplines: literature, languages, philosophy and religion, as well as history. Working with him gave great pleasure as well as broadening one's whole life.'[1]

Enoch Powell loathed Macmillan and Heath equally and it was a lifelong loathing. Heath and Macmillan, he wrote, were 'victims of their own propaganda'. Soon after Macmillan's death he wrote: 'Macmillan ... had no use for the Conservative loyalties and affections; they interfered too much with the Whig's true vocation of detecting trends in events and riding them skillfully so as to preserve the privileges, property and interests of his class.'[2]

In the battle for the soul of the Conservative Party, it seemed in the 1960s and 1970s that the likes of Macmillan and Heath had won hands down, and the harsh, uncompassionate conservatism of the 1930s had gone forever. But the mantle of Lord Salisbury was being picked up by a new sort of right-winger – not the scions of great houses, not the people who thought inheriting wealth was morally good in itself, but the people who thought making it was morally good in itself: people like Enoch Powell, Keith Joseph and Margaret Thatcher. The Macmillans and the Heaths were cast into the outer darkness, and it is only now, in 2005, that they seem to be making a comeback under the leadership of David Cameron.

His country changed greatly under Macmillan during his six years as Prime Minister, and he managed the change with great skill. But he did have some specific achievements to his credit. The nuclear test ban treaty was one, and both Kennedy and Khrushchev acknowledged that Macmillan's patient, skilful diplomacy was key to this. The Common Market application was an achievement too, even though it was ultimately unsuccessful. If Macmillan had not done the groundwork, on British public opinion, on the British political class, and on the leaders of Europe, then Wilson and Heath would have had to start much further back, and membership would have taken longer. Today almost no one thinks we ought to be outside Europe, but when Macmillan began, that was the mainstream view. In this Macmillan showed far more prescience than his three post-war predecessors, Attlee, Churchill and Eden.

But his biggest achievement was to manage the End of Empire: to realise that it had to be done, and to do it, in the teeth of furious charges of betrayal from his brothers-in-arms at Eton and Oxford, in the Grenadiers, in Churchill's wartime cabinet. He shares the honours with Clement Attlee, whose clear-sightedness set India and Burma free. Under Macmillan, Ghana and Malaya were granted independence in 1957,

## Macmillan's Premiership

'No modern premier, Churchill apart, ever brought such an eclectic experience to No. 10 along with his sovereign's commission. Macmillan really did have a sense of how his forbears had tackled the job. The Ghosts in the Cabinet Room were almost flesh and blood to him, as were the wraiths he saw in the House of Commons after his parliamentary triumphs – the spectres of the really brilliant figures who, unlike him, had not survived the Great War. It was, as a friend of his put it to me, almost as if he could hear the Raymond Asquiths and the Patrick Shaw-Stewarts saying, "What *you*, Harold – *you*, Prime Minister?"

How did this complicated, elusive man tackle the job? For all the touch of the country house about his No. 10, Cabinets were run tightly. He was very much in charge. To a recent analyst of his premiership, Richard Lamb, "The archives show that even more than generally believed Macmillan ran his government on the lines of an American President rather than a traditional British Prime Minister … Intellectually Macmillan towered head and shoulders above his Cabinet colleagues and, often mistrustful of their judgment, he insisted on full control … [he] interfered continuously with his colleagues' conduct of their departmental affairs."

Although not an Eden-style fusser, Macmillan was a shameless intervener in the business of his ministers, especially those he suspected of lacking dash or grip… . [A] favourite dismissive epithet was to call someone a 'good chief of staff.' When brigaded with the accusation of dullness it could make a truly damning condemnation. A classic example of this was when he was talking in the early 1980s to his official biographer, Alistair Horne, about Ted Heath: "… Hengist and Horsa were very dull people. Now, as you know, they colonized Kent [where Heath's constituency lay]; consequently the people of Kent have ever since been very slightly – well, you know … Ted was an excellent Chief Whip … a first class staff officer, but no army commander …"'

[Peter Hennessy, *The Prime Minister* (Penguin, London: 2000) pp 255–6.]

Nigeria in 1960 and Kenya in 1963. Rhodesia remained a problem for Wilson to grapple with, but Macmillan had established, in the teeth of furious opposition from his own backwoodsmen, a cross-party consensus that it was no longer acceptable to deny black people the vote. It may seem obvious to us now, but it was anything but obvious to most British people in 1957.

What of the debit side? In 1966 William Rees-Mogg wrote what became the standard right-wing view of Macmillan. 'Everyone knows that Mr Macmillan's real contributions ... are overshadowed by the failures of his last years, and the "never had it so good" election which prepared the way for those failures.'[3] This, for a time, became the standard criticism: that the supposed moral decay of the 1960s was somehow Macmillan's fault because he had encouraged people to think of material things. It was a very stupid criticism. It is the job of a Prime Minister to improve the material condition of the people, if he can, and only those who are too rich to care will complain when he does so, and thereby pleases the people. Later, the Thatcherites derided Macmillan's record because there were far too many areas where Labour and the Conservatives agreed. 'For me,' Margaret Thatcher said in 1981, 'consensus seems to be the process for abandoning all beliefs, principles, values and policies.' Unemployment was kept low and prices stable under Macmillan. The government worked with the unions, and living standards of ordinary people increased far more than under Thatcher.

Under another Prime Minister it might have been very different. 'From 1955 onward,' wrote Vernon Bogdanor, 'the British economy was bedevilled by a series of exchange crises which seemed to show that sterling could only be defended in a period of fixed exchange rates through strict control of the money supply. This was a policy favoured by Macmillan's first chancellor, Peter Thorneycroft, and by his junior ministers, Nigel Birch and Enoch Powell – the latter providing the doctrinal foundation for polices thought obsolete in the 1950s but newly-fashionable 20 years later. Macmillan was not impressed. *When I am told … that inflation can be cured or arrested only by returning to substantial or even massive unemployment, I reject that utterly.*'[4]

*When I am told … that inflation can be cured or arrested only by returning to substantial or even massive unemployment, I reject that utterly.*

MACMILLAN

Thorneycroft, Powell and Birch – the voices of what would later become known as Thatcherism – resigned, doing as much damage as they could on the way out, but not enough seriously to hurt Macmillan. When he said that most people had never had it so good, he was speaking the plain truth. Tory governments of the 1930s presided happily over mass unemployment, but Macmillan could not have done that.

His faults were those of a wealthy Edwardian gentleman – Eton, Oxford, the Grenadiers – dealing in his sixties with a world which was shaking off the habit of respect and deference to the well-born. Just as Macmillan represented something, so too did Peter Cook, and Macmillan could not understand what it was. What he was hearing from Peter Cook was the terrible sound of crumbling respect. The playwrights John Osborne and Arnold Wesker represented something too, and what they represented was even more alien to the elderly, patrician Prime Minister, whose private, rather rambling first thoughts on his successor branched out into a rant against modern drama. John Osborne's first play *Look Back in Anger* burst onto the London stage in 1956, and for the first time the London theatre started to talk about a class that Macmillan could idealise but could never understand.

For although he presided over it with dignity and

flexibility, he did not understand the decade over which he was presiding. The 1950s was the world of Dennis Potter's 'great greyness', the 'feeling of the flatness and bleakness of everyday England'. It was a world in which, as Jimmy Porter put it in *Look Back in Anger*, 'nobody thinks, nobody cares'; or, in the words of the young man about to go and fight in Suez in Osborne's next play, *The Entertainer*, 'things aren't that bad, and even if they are, there's nothing we can do about it.'

The 1960s did not invent liberalism, but they did democratise it. As the recent film *Vera Drake* showed, members of the upper classes in the 1950s could always get a safe abortion or a rapid divorce, carry on affairs, both heterosexual and homosexual, or get hold of a copy of *Lady Chatterley's Lover.* The point of the ban lay in the prosecution lawyer's famous remark at the Lady Chatterley trial: to keep it away from the servants. It was a world in which Lady Dorothy Macmillan could carry on an extra-marital affair and have a child by her lover, but a middle- or lower-class woman could not.

Macmillan was watching in some bewilderment the start of the long, lingering death of deference and class distinction. Today it seems to be being replaced with something else – overweening respect for anyone rich – but that is another question. He was a snob. Class distinction was to him one of the glories of his nation. He was pleased to be born rich, but he would really have liked it to be old money, not new money, and he was pleased to be able to marry into the old aristocracy, and acquire in-laws who would look down on him for being a parvenu. That snobbery played a part in the selection of Alec Douglas-Home as his successor, a decision which may (or may not) have cost the Conservative Party the 1964 election.

He was not at all unflappable. The popular perception

of unflappability came from a lifetime of knowing that a stiff upper lip was expected of an English gentleman, but it disguised a turmoil within. This should not surprise us. Remember him in the First World War – the young soldier whose insouciant bravery in walking up and down under fire so impressed his comrades? Are we to suppose he was not afraid? Only a stupid man would have no fear. He was scared witless. He was liable to quiet panic, but the expression on his face and the tone of his voice never showed it. It sometimes affected his judgement, which was dreadful over Suez, poor at the time of the night of the long knives, out of touch over Profumo, and erratic over the question of selecting his successor.

But despite all that, I count him as a great statesman, a great Prime Minister, and a decent and intelligent man with humane instincts. He once said of Margaret Thatcher: *I wish she'd read a book*. She said of him that as an eager young MP, she heard him explain 'that Prime Ministers (not having a department of their own) have plenty of spare time for reading. He recommended Disraeli and Trollope.' She 'sometimes wondered if he was joking'.[5] But he was not. He read and re-read, even at the busiest of times, and it kept him sane. Curiously, if he had to choose one book to re-read, it would have been the same one as Clement Attlee would have chosen: Jane Austen's *Pride and Prejudice*.

Here is the verdict I think he would like most, and I think he earned it. Harold Macmillan was a decent and humane man from the British upper classes, who fought bravely for his country during the First World War, and whose skill, diplomacy and courage made real contributions towards victory in the Second; who led his country through six difficult years, ensuring that most of his people were in work and starvation was considered a thing of the past; who mended the transatlantic relationship which was on the point of being fractured, and laid the seeds for a new relationship with Europe. Few Prime Ministers can claim so much.

# NOTES

## Chapter 1: The House of Macmillan (1894–1914)

1. Alastair Horne, *Macmillan*, Volume 1, 1894–1965 (Macmillan, London: 1988) p 14, hereafter Horne 1.
2. Simon Ball, *The Guardsmen* (HarperCollins, London: 2004) p 15.
3. Anthony Sampson, *Macmillan, A Study in Ambiguity* (Allen Lane, London: 1967) p 19.
4. Horne 1, p 31.
5. Evelyn Waugh, *The Life of the Right Revd Ronald Knox* (Chapman and Hall, London: 1959) pp 139–41.

## Chapter 2: The War that Changed Everything (1915–19)

1. Horne 1, p 36.
2. Horne 1, p 40.
3. Ball, *The Guardsmen*, p 54.
4. Horne 1, p 43.
5. *The Times*, 18 October 1975.
6. Hugh Dalton, *Call Back Yesterday* (Muller, London: 1953) p 102.

## Chapter 3: Years of Hope and Despair (1919–29)

1. Horne 1, p 57.
2. Ball, *The Guardsmen*, p 95.
3. Harold Macmillan, *Winds of Change* (volume one of the autobiography) (Macmillan, London: 1966).
4. Ball, *The Guardsmen*, p 99.
5. Sampson, *Macmillan*, p 28.

6. Horne 1, p 78.
7. Cherie Booth and Cate Haste, *The Goldfish Bowl – Married to the Prime Minister, 1955–97* (Chatto and Windus, London: 2004) p 42.

### Chapter 4: The Coming of Another War (1929–39)

1. Francis Beckett, *Clem Attlee* (Richard Cohen Books, London: 2000) p 98.
2. Cuthbert Headlam, *The Headlam Diaries* (ed. Stuart Ball) (Cambridge: 1999).
3. *Star*, 20 March 1936.
4. Sampson, *Macmillan*, p 57.

### Chapter 5: The Ruler of the Mediterranean (1940–5)

1. Winston S Churchill, *The Second World War Volume 1: The Gathering Storm* (Cassell, London: 1948) pp 525–6.
2. Andrew Roberts, *Eminent Churchillians* (Weidenfeld & Nicolson, London: 1994) p 138.
3. Ball, *The Guardsmen*, pp 220–1.
4. Herbert Morrison, *An Autobiography* (Odhams Press, London: 1960) p 300.
5. Horne 1, p 145.
6. Ball, *The Guardsmen*, p 256.
7. Ruth Dudley Edwards, *Harold Macmillan* (Macmillan, London: 1983) p 63.
8. Harold Macmillan, *War Diaries: The Mediterranean 1943–5* (Macmillan, London: 1984).
9. Edwards, *Harold Macmillan*, p 69.
10. Headlam, *Diaries*, p 468.

### Chapter 6: Attlee and Churchill remake Britain (1945–55)

1. Beckett, *Clem Attlee*, p 296.

2. Harold Macmillan, *Diaries: The Cabinet Years* (ed. Peter Catterall) (Macmillan, London: 2003) p 64.
3. Macmillan, *Diaries: The Cabinet Years*, p 114.
4. Horne 1, p 359.
5. Edwards, *Harold Macmillan*, p 73.
6. John Charmley, *A History of Conservative Politics* (Macmillan, London: 1996) p 153.
7. Horne 1, p 360.
8. Horne 1, p 361.

### Chapter 7: 'Wab or Hawold?' (1956)

All quotes from Macmillan in this chapter are from Macmillan, *Diaries: The Cabinet Years*, unless otherwise stated.

1. Horne 1, p 381.
2. Peter Hennessy, *The Prime Minister – The Office and its Holders* (Penguin, London: 2000), p 207.
3. Nigel Fisher, *Harold Macmillan, A Biography* (Weidenfeld & Nicolson, London: 1982).
4. Ball, *The Guardsmen*, p 326.

### Chapter 8: Plucking Victory from the Jaws of Defeat (1957–60)

1. Robert Blake, *The Conservative Party from Peel to Major* (Heinemann, London: 1997) p 273.
2. Macmillan, *Diaries: The Cabinet Years*, p 613.
3. Ball, *The Guardsmen*, pp 328–9.
4. Horne, pp 451–2.
5. Richard Lamb, *The Macmillan Years – The Emerging Truth* (John Murray, London: 1995) p 27.
6. Charmley, *A History of Conservative Politics*, p 160.
7. Lamb, *The Macmillan Years – The Emerging Truth*, p 47.
8. Lamb, *The Macmillan Years – The Emerging Truth*, p 51.
9. Simon Heffer, *Like the Roman – the life of Enoch Powell*

(Weidenfeld & Nicolson, London: 1998) p 324.
10. Heffer, *Like the Roman*, p 324.

### Chapter 9: Plucking Defeat from the Jaws of Victory (1959–63)

1. Alastair Horne, *Macmillan*, Volume 2, 1966–1986 (Macmillan, London: 1989) p 178, hereafter Horne 2.
2. *The Spectator*, 17 January 1964.
3. Horne 2, p 186.
4. Ball, *The Guardsmen*, p 355.
5. Sampson, *Macmillan*, pp 185–7.
6. Lamb, *The Macmillan Years – The Emerging Truth*, p 81.
7. Heffer, *Like the Roman*, p 301.
8. D R Thorpe, *Selwyn Lloyd* (Cape, London: 1989) p 343.
9. D R Thorpe, *Alec Douglas-Home* (Sinclair Stevenson, London: 1996) p 257.
10. Peter Riddell, *Hug Them Close* (Politico's, London: 2003) p 55.
11. Bernard Levin, *Run It Down the Flagpole* (Cape, London: 1970), pp 63–4, 76.
12. Thorpe, *Douglas-Home*, p 296.
13. Thorpe, *Douglas-Home*, pp 301–2.

### Chapter 10: 'Selling the family silver' (1963–86)

1. Roberts, *Eminent Churchillians*, p 258.

### Chapter 11: The Last Edwardian, the First Moderniser

1. Edward Heath, *The Course of My Life* (Hodder and Stoughton, London: 1998).
2. Heffer, *Like the Roman*, p 210.
3. William Rees-Mogg, *The Sunday Times*, 3 April 1966.
4. Vernon Bogdanor, *The Guardian*, 30 December 1986.
5. Hennessy, *The Prime Minister*, p 271.

# CHRONOLOGY

| Year | Premiership |
|---|---|
| *1957* | 10 January: Exactly a month before his 63rd birthday Harold Macmillan becomes Prime Minister. Appoints Rab Butler as Home Secretary, Selwyn Lloyd as Foreign Secretary and Thorneycroft as Chancellor of the Exchequer.<br>Lord Salisbury resigns as Leader of the Lords over Cyprus.<br>Eisenhower and Macmillan re-establish the 'special relationship' which had been strained by the Suez crisis.<br>Wolfenden Report on homosexuality and prostitution published. |
| *1958* | Britain announces new plans for Cyprus, involving representatives of the Greek and Turkish governments in the island's administration. |

| History | Culture |
| --- | --- |
| Belgium, France, West Germany, Italy, Luxembourg and Netherlands sign Treaty of Rome establishing the European Economic Community (EEC).<br>USA, Britain, France and West Germany issue declaration on principles of German reunification and call for free elections.<br>Sweeping victory for Konrad Adenauer in West German elections. | Kenneth Clark, *The Nude.*<br>Jack Kerouac, *On the Road.*<br>Patrick White, *Voss.*<br>Samuel Beckett, *Endgame.*<br>Bernstein, *West Side Story.*<br>Poulenc, *Les Dialogues des Carmelites* (opera).<br>Francis Bacon, *Screaming Nurse.*<br>John Osborne, *The Entertainer.*<br>Films: *The Bridge on the River Kwai. The Prince and the Showgirl.*<br>TV: *The Sky at Night.* First television broadcast of the Queen's Christmas Day message. |
| European Economic Community and European Atomic Energy Commission in force.<br>Treaty signed at the Hague by Belgium, Netherlands and Luxembourg establishing 'Benelux' Economic Union.<br>In USSR Khrushchev replaces Bulganin as premier.<br>Khrushchev withdraws previous support for UN Security Council meeting and proposes meeting of UN General Assembly which is accepted by USA and Britain.<br>Charles de Gaulle elected president of French Republic. | Wittgenstein, *The Blue Book. The Brown Book* (posthumous).<br>Iris Murdoch, *The Bell.*<br>Boris Pasternak, *Dr Zhivago.*<br>Harold Pinter, *The Birthday Party.*<br>Johnson and van der Rohe, Seagram Building New York.<br>Arnold Wesker, *Chicken Soup with Barley.*<br>Benjamin Britten, *Noye's Fludde.*<br>Perry Como, *Magic Moments.*<br>Films: *Gigi. Touch of Evil. Vertigo.*<br>TV: *Blue Peter. Grandstand.* |

| Year | Premiership |
| --- | --- |
| *1959* | Agreement signed in London by Prime Ministers of Greece, Turkey and Britain for independence of Cyprus.<br>Resignations of Chancellor Thorneycroft, Nigel Birch and Enoch Powell over economic policy dismissed as *these little local difficulties* by Macmillan.<br>Disturbances in British territory of Nyasaland (Malawi); state of emergency is declared. Conservatives win general election, with 365 seats to Labour's 258. |
| *1960* | Macmillan visits Ghana, Nigeria, Rhodesia and South Africa. Makes *Wind of Change* speech in Cape Town.<br>In Britain, the Labour Party conference votes in favour of unilateral nuclear disarmament<br>Summit meeting in Paris between Khrushchev, Macmillan, Eisenhower and de Gaulle. Khrushchev breaks up summit because Eisenhower refuses to apologise for invasion of Soviet airspace by a US spy aircraft earlier in the year. |

| History | Culture |
| --- | --- |
| Liu Shaoqi elected chairman of Chinese Republic in succession to Mao Zedong.<br>UN votes against admission of People's Republic of China.<br>UN General Assembly condemns apartheid in South Africa and all other racial discrimination.<br>Conference in Stockholm, Finance ministers of Austria, Denmark, Britain, Norway, Portugal, Sweden and Switzerland establish European Free Trade Association.<br>Britain and Arab Republic (Syria and Egypt) resume diplomatic relations. | Saul Bellow, *Henderson the Rain King.*<br>Günther Grass, *The Tin Drum.*<br>Brendan Behan, *The Hostage.*<br>Harold Pinter, *The Caretaker.*<br>Frank Lloyd Wright, Beth Shalom Synagogue, Pennsylvania.<br>Francis Poulenc, *La voix humaine* (opera).<br>Rodgers/Hammerstein, *The Sound of Music.*<br>Motown Records founded in Detroit, USA.<br>Films: *Ben Hur. Some Like it Hot. North by Northwest.* |
| Sharpeville Massacre in South Africa: during a demonstration police panic and kill 69, injure 186. Following strikes, demonstrations and marches, state of emergency is proclaimed in South Africa.<br>European Free Trade Association comes into force.<br>Brezhnev replaces Voroshilov as president of USSR.<br>Democrat John F Kennedy wins US presidential election.<br>OECD treaty signed in Paris by USA, Canada and 18 member countries of OEEC. | AJ Ayer, *Logical Positivism.*<br>John Updike, *Rabbit Run.*<br>Alain Robbe-Grillet, *Dans la labyrinthe.*<br>Robert Bolt, *A Man for All Seasons.*<br>Frank Lloyd Wright, Guggenheim Museum, New York.<br>Benjamin Britten, *A Midsummer Night's Dream.*<br>Lionel Bart, *Oliver!.*<br>Films: *The Magnificent Seven. Psycho. Saturday Night and Sunday Morning.*<br>TV: *Coronation Street.* |

| Year | Premiership |
| --- | --- |
| *1961* | Britain applies for membership of the European Economic Community.<br>*Private Eye* magazine founded. |
| *1962* | Britain applies to join European Coal and Steel Community and Euratom<br>July: Macmillan sacks Chancellor Selwyn Lloyd and six other ministers in so-called 'Night of the Long Knives'. |

| History | Culture |
| --- | --- |
| USA severs diplomatic relations with Cuba.<br>Prime Minister Verwoerd announces that South Africa will leave the British Commonwealth osn 31 May.<br>Khrushchev proposes German peace conference to President Kennedy.<br>USA and USSR begin disarmament talks in Washington DC.<br>Construction of the the Berlin Wall.<br>Army coup in Damascus, Syria. Syria secedes from United Arab Republic and forms Syrian Arab Republic. | Jean Anouilh, *Becket.*<br>John Osborne, *Luther.*<br>In London, Hardwick's neo-classical arch at Euston Station is demolished.<br>British cellist Jacqueline du Pré makes her solo debut at age 16.<br>Henry Mancini, *Moon River.*<br>Elvis Presley, *Are you lonesome tonight?*.<br>The Rolling Stones form.<br>The Beatles debut in Liverpool.<br>Films: *Breakfast at Tiffany's. West Side Story. Victim.*<br>TV: *The Avengers*. |
| France proclaims independence of Algeria.<br>USSR agrees to send arms to Cuba.<br>Start of the Cuban Missile Crisis, Kennedy announces that the USSR has installed a missile base in Cuba and calls on Khrushchev to eliminate this threat to world peace.<br>Khrushchev writes to Kennedy saying he will remove weapons 'regarded as offensive' if USA removes its missiles from Turkey. Kennedy rejects this, insisting work on missile bases in Cuba must stop. Later, Kennedy announces that USSR is dismantling these bases.<br>USSR agrees to withdraw Ilyushin bombers from Cuba and USA announces end of blockade. | Anthony Sampson, *The Anatomy of Britain.*<br>Alexander Solzhenitsyn, *One day in the Life of Ivan Denisovich.*<br>Edward Albee, *Who's afraid of Virginia Woolf?*<br>Basil Spence's Coventry Cathedral is consecrated.<br>Benjamin Britten, *War Requiem.*<br>Michael Tippet, *King Priam.*<br>Bob Dylan, *Blowing in the Wind.*<br>The Beatles, *Love Me Do*.<br>Films: *The Birds. Lawrence of Arabia. Lolita. The Loneliness of the Long Distance Runner. Dr No.*<br>TV: *That Was the Week that Was. University Challenge.* |

| Year | Premiership |
|---|---|
| *1963* | De Gaulle states objections to Britain joining EEC. Later, Britain's entry is refused.<br>Britain and USA sign Polaris missile agreement.<br>John Profumo resigns from the government, admitting that he misled the House of Commons over his relationship with Christine Keeler.<br>USA, USSR and Britain sign nuclear test ban treaty, subsequently signed by 96 countries.<br>18 October: Macmillan resigns after six years and 281 days in office. |

| History | Culture |
|---|---|
| Geneva conference of General Agreement on Tariffs and Trade begins 'Kennedy round' of negotiations for tariff cuts.<br>Agreement to establish a 'hot line' between White House, Washington DC and Kremlin, Moscow.<br>Kennedy visits West Berlin and gives 'Ich bin ein Berliner' speech.<br>In USA, African-Americans take part in peaceful demonstration for civil rights. Martin Luther King gives 'I have a dream …' speech. | Eugene Ionesco, *Exit the King.*<br>John Le Carré, *The Spy Who Came in from the Cold.*<br>Le Corbusier, Carpenter Center for the Visual Arts, Harvard University, USA.<br>Gerry and the Pacemakers, *You'll never walk alone.*<br>The Beatles, *Please Please me. She loves you. I want to hold your hand.*<br>Films: *The Great Escape. Cleopatra. Tom Jones.*<br>TV: *Dr Who. World in Action.* |

# FURTHER READING

The next staging-post, for the reader who wants to understand a little more about Macmillan, could well be *The Guardsmen* by Simon Ball (HarperCollins, London: 2004), a racily-written book which contains some of the most up-to-date research. Subtitled *Harold Macmillan, three friends, and the world they made*, it traces the lives of four men who went to Eton together in 1906, joined the Grenadiers and fought in the First World War together, went into Conservative politics together, and entered the government together in 1940 under Winston Churchill: Macmillan, Oliver Lyttelton, Bobbety Cranborne and Harry Crookshank. It describes the British ruling class in the 20th century, and is luminously written and full of unexpected insights into the way these men thought, lived, and ran the country.

It helps fill a gap; for although his premiership was pivotal, and he was a fascinating and in some ways rather sad figure, Harold Macmillan has not attracted the sort of attention from biographers you might have expected. Maybe that is because left-wing writers prefer writing about Labour politicians, and right-wing writers see him as a traitor to the cause.

For lucid and elegant expositions of the 'traitor' view – in which Macmillan is one of the worst in a long line of leaders who have sold conservatism down the river, stretching at least back to Churchill if not to Baldwin – see John Charmley's *A History of Conservative Politics 1900–96* (Macmillan, London: 1996) or Andrew Roberts's *Eminent Churchillians* (Weidenfeld & Nicolson, London: 1994). For a rather more measured assessment of Macmillan's place in Conservative Party history, try *The Conservative Party from Peel to Major* by Robert Blake (Heinemann, London: 1997).

Another reason biographers avoid Macmillan may be that the official job was so well done. Alastair Horne's two-volume *Macmillan* (Macmillan, London: 1988/89) is both authoritative and readable. It is also massive – a total of 1,300 pages or so – which makes it a book almost exclusively for the index and contents list reader. By contrast, *Harold Macmillan* (Weidenfeld & Nicolson, London: 1982) by fellow Conservative politician and old Etonian, Sir Nigel Fisher, is prim and loyal at the expense of being informative. It contains, for example, no mention at all of Lady Dorothy Macmillan's affair with Robert Boothby, though this was one of the most important events in Macmillan's life. The early biography by Anthony Sampson – *Macmillan, A Study in Ambiguity* (Allen Lane, London: 1967) – remains a thoughtful and interesting book, few of whose judgements have been rendered idiotic by the passing of the years.

Material on Macmillan's government not available to Horne and Fisher was marshalled by Richard Lamb for his book *The Macmillan Years 1957–63* (John Murray, London: 1995). It is another big book – 500+ pages – and the cover, with the sinister subtitle *The Emerging Truth*, seems to promise revelations the book does not deliver. It does not, in fact, seriously challenge the Horne verdicts, though adding some detail unavailable to Horne.

Other books I have found particularly useful in this study are: *Alec Douglas-Home* by D R Thorpe (Sinclair-Stevenson, London: 1996); *An Affair of State – The Profumo Case and the Framing of Stephen Ward* by Phillip Knightley and Caroline Kennedy (Cape, London: 1987); *Winds of Change – The End of Empire in Africa* by Trevor Royle (John Murray, London: 1996); *Like the Roman – The Life of Enoch Powell* by Simon

Heffer (Weidenfeld & Nicolson, London: 1998); and of course Peter Hennessy's magisterial *The Prime Minister – The Office and its Holders Since 1945* (Penguin, London: 2000).

Of course the serious student will also want Macmillan's own entertaining and often sardonic diaries, edited by Peter Catterall and only now starting to emerge – the first volume is *The Macmillan Diaries – the Cabinet Years, 1950–7* (Macmillan, London: 2003). There are also the six huge volumes of his memoirs – *Winds of Change* (Macmillan, London: 1966), *The Blast of War* (Macmillan, London: 1967), *Tides of Fortune* (Macmillan, London: 1969), *Riding the Storm* (Macmillan, London: 1971), *Pointing the Way* (Macmillan, London: 1971) and *At the End of the Day* (Macmillan, London:1972).

# PICTURE SOURCES

Page vi–vii
Harold Macmillan indulging in a favourite pastime, grouse-shooting in Yorkshire, 1964.
(Courtesy Topham Picturepoint)

Page 82–3
President Kennedy listening to a welcoming speech by Harold Macmillan after his arrival at Gatwick airport, 29 June 1963. (Courtesy Topham Picturepoint)

Page 129
An official photographic portrait of Harold Macmillan taken in 1960. (Courtesy akg Images)

# INDEX

## D



## E



## F



## G

# THE 20 BRITISH PRIME MINISTERS OF THE 20TH CENTURY

## SALISBURY

Conservative politician, prime minister 1885–6, 1886–92 and 1895–1902, and the last to hold that office in the House of Lords.

by Eric Midwinter

Visiting Professor of Education at Exeter University

ISBN 1-904950-54-X (pb)

## BALFOUR

Balfour wrote that Britain favoured 'the establishment in Palestine of a national home for the Jewish people', the so-called 'Balfour Declaration'.

by Ewen Green

of Magdalen College Oxford

ISBN 1-904950-55-8 (pb)

## CAMPBELL-BANNERMAN

Liberal Prime Minister, who started the battle with the Conservative-dominated House of Lords.

by Lord Hattersley

former Deputy Leader of the Labour Party and Cabinet member in Wilson and Callaghan's governments.

ISBN 1-904950-56-6 (pb)

## ASQUITH

His administration laid the foundation of Britain's welfare state, but he was plunged into a major power struggle with the House of Lords.

by Stephen Bates

a senior correspondent for the *Guardian.*

ISBN 1-904950-57-4 (pb)

## LLOYD GEORGE

By the end of 1916 there was discontent with Asquith's management of the war, and Lloyd George schemed secretly with the Conservatives in the coalition government to take his place.

by Hugh Purcell

television documentary maker.

ISBN 1-904950-58-2 (pb)

## BONAR LAW

In 1922 he was the moving spirit in the stormy meeting of Conservative MPs which ended the coalition, created the 1922 Committee and reinstated him as leader.

by Andrew Taylor

Professor of Politics at the University of Sheffield.

ISBN 1-904950-59-0 (pb)

## BALDWIN

Baldwin's terms of office included two major political crises, the General Strike and the Abdication.

by Anne Perkins

a journalist, working mostly for the *Guardian*, as well as a historian of the British labour movement.

ISBN 1-904950-60-4 (pb)

## MACDONALD

In 1900 he was the first secretary of the newly formed Labour Representation Committee (the original name for the Labour party). Four years later he became the first Labour prime minister.

### by Kevin Morgan

who teaches government and politics at Manchester University.

ISBN 1-904950-61-2 (pb)

## CHAMBERLAIN

His name will forever be linked to the policy of appeasement and the Munich agreement he reached with Hitler.

### by Graham Macklin

manager of the research service at the National Archives.

ISBN 1-904950-62-0 (pb)

## CHURCHILL

Perhaps the most determined and inspirational war leader in Britain's history.

### by Chris Wrigley

who has written about David Lloyd George, Arthur Henderson and W E Gladstone.

ISBN 1-904950-63-9 (pb)

## ATTLEE

His post-war government enacted a broad programme of socialist legislation in spite of conditions of austerity. His legacy: the National Health Service.

### by David Howell

Professor of Politics at the University of York and an expert in Labour's history.

ISBN 1-904950-64-7 (pb)

## EDEN

His premiership will forever be linked to the fateful Suez Crisis.

by Peter Wilby

former editor of the *New Statesman*.

ISBN 1-904950-65-5 (pb)

## MACMILLAN

He repaired the rift between the USA and Britain created by Suez and secured for Britain co-operation on issues of nuclear defence, but entry into the EEC was vetoed by de Gaulle in 1963.

by Francis Beckett

author of BEVAN, published by Haus in 2004.

ISBN 1-904950-66-3 (pb)

## DOUGLAS-HOME

Conservative politician and prime minister 1963-4, with a complex career between the two Houses of Parliament.

by David Dutton

who teaches History at Liverpool University.

ISBN 1-904950-67-1 (pb)

## WILSON

He held out the promise progress, of 'the Britain that is going to be forged in the white heat of this revolution'. The forced devaluation of the pound in 1967 frustrated the fulfilment of his promises.

by Paul Routledge

The *Daily Mirror's* chief political commentator.

ISBN 1-904950-68-X (pb)

## HEATH

A passionate European, he succeeded during his premiership in effecting Britain's entry to the EC.

by Denis MacShane

Minister for Europe in Tony Blair's first government.

ISBN 1-904950-69-8 (pb)

## CALLAGHAN

His term in office was dominated by industrial unrest, culminating in the 'Winter of Discontent'.

by Harry Conroy

When James Callaghan was Prime Minister, Conroy was the Labour Party's press officer in Scotland, and he is now editor of the Scottish *Catholic Observer.*

ISBN 1-904950-70-1 (pb)

## THATCHER

Britain's first woman prime minister and the longest serving head of government in the 20th century (1979–90), but also the only one to be removed from office in peacetime by pressure from within her own party.

by Clare Beckett

teaches social policy at Bradford University.

ISBN 1-904950-71-X (pb)

## MAJOR

He enjoyed great popularity in his early months as prime minister, as he seemed more caring than his iron predecessor, but by the end of 1992 nothing seemed to go right.

by Robert Taylor

is Research Associate at the LSE's Centre for Economic Performance.

ISBN 1-904950-72-8 (pb)

## BLAIR

He is therefore the last prime minister of the 20th century and one of the most controversial ones, being frequently accused of abandoning cabinet government and introducing a presidential style of leadership.

by Mick Temple

is a senior lecturer in Politics and Journalism at Staffordshire University.

ISBN 1-904950-73-6 (pb)

THE 20 BRITISH PRIME MINISTERS
OF THE 20TH CENTURY

www.hauspublishing.co.uk

## DE GAULLE

by Julian Jackson

ISBN 1-904341-44-6 (pb)

Charles de Gaulle, saviour of France's honour in 1940 and founder of the Fifth Republic in 1958, was a man of contradictions. A conservative who brought the communists into his government and an imperialist who completed France's decolonisation. As Julian Jackson shows, it waas precisely because of these contradictions that de Gaulle was able to unite the French people behind a political system for the first time since the Revolution.

In British political history he is remembered for his clashes with Churchill during World War Two. When Churchill attacked him: 'You say you are France! You are not France! I did not recognize you as France.' De Gaulle responded: 'Why are you discussing these questions with me if I am not France … I am acting in the name of France. I am fighting alongside England. I am not fighting for England.' De Gaulle's experience during the war had convinced him that it would be difficult to drive a wedge between Britain and America. He frequently returned to a remark that Churchill had allegedly made to him on the eve of the Normandy landings: 'each time we must choose between Europe and the open sea, we shall always choose the open sea. Each time I must choose between you and Roosevelt, I shall choose Roosevelt.' It is not surprising, therefore, that de Gaulle vetoed the British application to join the Common Market which the Macmillan government made. The General called for a 'European Europe', a western-European bloc free of foreign (that is, American) domination.

## MOSLEY

by Nigel Jones

ISBN 1-904341-09-8 (pb)

Oswald Mosley was Britain's failed Führer. His political career began brilliantly: standing as a Conservative candidate he became the youngest Member of Parliament of his day. He soon changed his allegiance, convincingly pleading the Labour cause and sharing a Merseyside platform with the transport union boss and future Foreign Secretary Ernest Bevin. John Strachey, Aneurin Bevan and Allan Young composed a document, the 'Mosley Manifesto', stating the case for a small emergency Cabinet, public works and protectionism towards home industries. Mosley was winning over not just Labour supporters, but also disaffected Tories and Liberals. 'As Mosley basked in a warm glow of popular approval, Tory friends such as Boothby, Macmillan and Walter Elliott fired off letters of support to the press', writes Nigel Jones. 'But beneath all this Labourism, the whiff of fascism was in the air.' Mosley, as his biographer Robert Skidelsky records, was already in the mood to take 'the first tentative steps that were to lead him to fascism' and the founding of the notorious 'Blackshirts': the British Union of Fascists, secretly funded by Mussolini but increasingly influenced by the Nazis. Released from prison after the war, Mosley tried to refound his movement from exile in France, attacking Britain's new immigrants and advocating a united white Europe.

This is the first biography of Mosley since his death in 1980 and makes full use of recent research into British fascism. Race, nation and political violence are urgent issues throughout Europe today: Nigel Jones's analysis of Mosley's appeal, and his failure, is vital reading.

# BEVAN

by Clare & Francis Beckett

ISBN 1-904341-63-2 (pb)

'I tell you, it's the Labour Party or nothing!' said Nye Bevan to his wife, Jennie Lee, in 1931. That is the key to the politician Bevan was, say Clare Beckett and Francis Beckett in their biography of the man who more than anyone instituted Britain's welfare state. Personality politics were not Bevan's politics. He was a rebel, but a reluctant rebel. That may have saved Bevan from the kind of eventual isolation that is often the lot of natural, charismatic rebels. Perhaps it also lost him the chance to lead the Labour Party: when it came to it, Bevan was not ready enough to intrigue on behalf of himself.

He was a miner's son who became a miner himself, who saw his father die in his arms with his lungs full of coal dust, who knew exactly what poverty and powerlessness meant. These were scarring, driving experiences. He was also an astringent critic of much that smacked to him of accommodation and compromise in the Labour Party. He managed to get himself expelled from the Party once, and came near to it a second time, a considerable achievement for a reluctant rebel.

Perhaps he alienated colleagues by having what Denis Healey famously called 'a hinterland' – dimensions to his personal life that were not strictly political. In politics, such dimensions are liable to evoke suspicion. In 1945 the new Prime Minister Clement Atlee 'gave Bevan a real job to do and he did it brilliantly,' say his biographers. The result was planned local authority housing and the National Health Service.